Peter Shaffer

Equus

edited by
T S Pearce

with a personal essay by
Peter Shaffer

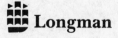
Longman

LONGMAN GROUP LIMITED
Longman House
Burnt Mill, Harlow, Essex CM20 2JE, England and
Associated Companies throughout the World

This edition first published in Longman Study Texts 1983
in association with André Deutsch Limited

ISBN 0 582 33129 3

Set in 10/12pt. Linotron 202 Baskerville
by Syarikat Seng Teik Sdn. Bhd., Kuala Lumpur

Printed in Hong Kong by
Wing Tai Cheung Printing Co Ltd

Contents

A personal essay by Peter Shaffer   vi

Introduction

Too close for comfort?   xi
Is 'theatre' literature?   xii
Is *Equus* realistic?   xiii
Can you believe it?   xiii
The ideal and the practical   xvii
A note on the language   xviii
A note on the author   xix

Equus   1

Notes   95

Follow-up work and questions for discussion   108

A personal essay

by Peter Shaffer

An introduction to three plays: The Royal Hunt of the Sun, Equus *and* Amadeus

It is hard for me to comment on these plays. I do not much like the idea of an author, as it were, walking along beside his texts, pointing out features of interest in them. As a matter of fact, I do not much like anybody else doing so: as I grow older I confess that I have less and less use for criticism, exegesis, or scholarly essays of explication. In America, where I have spent a fair portion of my time, writing seems to have fallen almost entirely into the hands of commentators.

The pages of this volume contain the material of live theatre. They are of no use to the radio director, the television director, even the cinema director. The material is intended to be brought to physical life in a space which has to be animated afresh each time of playing, by the vibrations of the actors and by those of the spectators. A play, like justice, is pre-eminently a thing *seen* to be done.

This is why, I hope, these three plays possess certain features in common. Each owns a certain flamboyance: a reliance upon gesture to enshrine idea – without which there is no theatre; a desire to enthral a crowd of watchers – without which there is certainly no theatre; and a strong pleasure in illusion. I imagine that this pleasure has always been a motive with me, ever since as a young boy I laid out a pack of cards on my pillow in bed, and imagined the lives of the Kings, Queens and Jacks rather than play games with them.

It is my object to tell tales; to conjure the spectres of horror and happiness, and fill other heads with the images which have haunted my own. My desire, I suppose, is to perturb and make gasp: to please and make laugh: to surprise. If I am a peacock in this respect, at least I am aware that peacockery is one of the dramatist's obligations. 'Don't show off' is not an adjuration to be made sensibly to playwrights. Needless to say, this does not exonerate in me, or in any writer, excessive spreading of tail-feathers.

The Royal Hunt of the Sun, the earliest of the three, was produced most splendidly by John Dexter and the National Theatre at the Chichester Festival of 1964. Speaking of tail-feathers, I think that this celebrated production used up the entire (and considerable) stock of Chinese pheasant feathers available in England at that time. It was a hugely lavish affair, superbly set and costumed by Michael Annals. The colour supplements of two Sunday newspapers in London devoted astonished articles to its lavishness: this sort of spectacle had not been seen on drab English stages for some while. Audiences responded in tremendous and delighted numbers. To this day I still receive communications from people telling me how they can never forget the opening of the great metal sun near the beginning of the play, or the flood of blood red cloth vomiting out of it later to engulf them in the idea of massacre, or the golden funeral masks of the Incas, with their triangular eyes and copper cheeks, turned yearningly towards the rising sun at the end. This was not lavishness for the sake of it: lavishness was the point. Peru was a kingdom, wrote one mediaeval commentator, where gold was as common as wood in Spain. There was clearly no showing a kingdom of infinite treasures without recourse to some visual splendour. Similarly there was no creating the aural world of sixteenth-century Peru without a strange and continuing music. Many of my plays have used music, but none more elaborately than *The Royal Hunt of the Sun*. In my view, Marc Wilkinson's superb score is integral to the play.

Of course I do not mean to imply by any of the above that the words are not important. They are paramount. *The Royal Hunt of the Sun* took me three years to write. So did *Equus*. So did *Amadeus*. I write and destroy the writing; and rewrite, and destroy the rewriting – and I continue in this way until not only the images but the words are entirely clear in my mind, and the flavour of each scene is strong on my tongue. Each play has obviously to acquire a different kind of flavour – the three under discussion here are, after all, set in mediaeval Peru, modern Hampshire, and Enlightenment Vienna respectively; but all are obviously contemporary pieces in the sense that they were written by me and are being read by you.

Equus is obviously less rhetorical than *The Royal Hunt of the Sun*, but many of the same elements appear in it. Again there are masks, only they are now transparent: we see the actor's head through the wire head of the horse – a double image which is the preoccupation of the play. Once again there are raised boots, as in ancient theatre: the Inca in *Royal Hunt* appears before the massacre poised on huge *cothurni*; the horses stalk and stamp round their English stable on high metal hooves. The sound of their feet on the wooden stage, discreetly and alarmingly used, filled the theatre when the play was first produced at the National Theatre in 1973 (again by John Dexter) with an ominous scraping which seemed to herald divine presence. Once more there was music by Marc Wilkinson, this time an eerie humming in twelve tones to recall – in the composer's intention – Vienna, the city of Freud. Perhaps this last was a tenuous connection. All the same the play, as it grew under my hands, came more and more to question the ultimate uses of psychiatry. In the first draft the doctor was drawn more vaguely; less in the central position. In the second draft he grew more prominent, and his self-doubts more important to the meaning of the piece. In London *Equus* caused a sensation because it displayed cruelty to horses; in New York because it allegedly displayed cruelty to psychiatrists.

Of all my plays *Equus* was the most private. I wrote it for myself. I had no notion how popular it was to become – its extraordinary run of well over a thousand performances on Broadway could never have been remotely envisaged by me.

The play has been subject to a vast amount of commentary and misuse: a few doctors declaring it a madman's charter; some do-your-own-thingers using it as a means to justify every kind of human aberration. For me it is a deeply erotic play, and also one of tragic conflict. Tragedy obviously does not lie in a conflict of Right and Wrong, but in a collision between two different kinds of Right: in this case, surely, between Dysart's professional obligation to treat a terrified boy who has committed a dreadful crime, and Alan's passionate capacity for worship – his profound desire to cry 'O Magnum Mysterium!' alone in a rubbish-strewn field, his burning ecstasy set against his doctor's careful prosaicism. Dysart has to do what he does. Let no man say 'Do your own thing', for example, to Jack the Ripper. Yet in proceeding by his best and honourable lights, the doctor cannot but know that he is in some clear sense the destroyer of a passion he must forever, and rightly, envy.

Envy, of course, is also the theme of *Amadeus*: Salieri's envy of Mozart's genius. Again I have little to add about this play: what I needed to say on the theme of man's proper objection to divine arbitrariness seems to me to be fairly contained in the work itself. Of course Salieri commits a stupid sin – and I do not mean his persecution of Mozart. He demands a God he can understand. What artist would do that? He says, in effect, 'Let me dip my net into the unfathomable well, and bring up shining creatures hitherto unseen!' But he also says, 'Let me see to the bottom of this well: it is my right as a man! I object to the darkness wherein the connections of beauty are formed.' As well object to the dark of the womb! Confronted by divine mystery, he says merely, 'How dare you?' A fool, you say. And yet he also has his right. (Again the collision of 'Rights'.) All he wanted was to serve. To be owned by an Absolute. We need an answer for his torment. True he is condemned to chew forever the cud of his own poisonous sense of fairness – but yet who would dare say that a sense of fairness is dispensable?

Paul Scofield played Salieri at the National Theatre in

November 1979, and in New York Ian McKellen played the same part a year later, somewhat rewritten. The reasons for the changes, which were approved by audiences and critics who saw both versions, are explained in my preface to the new edition of the play.

In the end, I suppose, all three pieces share a common preoccupation with worship and man's attempts to acquire or murder a special divinity. This must indicate, surely, my own belief in its utter indispensability to our lives.

Introduction

Equus is a shocking play, in the proper sense of the word. It sets out to shock. When Martin Dysart asks Hesther Salomon what Alan Strang has done to need psychiatric treatment and makes a bad joke about dosing 'some little girl's Pepsi with Spanish Fly', Hesther's reply 'He blinded six horses with a metal spike' is so unexpected and so disgusting that even audiences hardened to the conventional horrors of war stories and thrillers are likely to feel some sort of jolt. This shock is precisely calculated and the play continues to produce shocks and surprises all the way through.

Too close for comfort?

Equus is also a very frank play. The inner, usually secret lives of the two central characters are exposed with clinical directness. It is a play about Martin Dysart and Alan Strang; but if you want to give it an abstract subject, then it is a play about religion and sex, or sex and religion, according to where you place the greater emphasis. These topics, if not actually embarrassing, are certainly not easy for many people to discuss openly, although in one way or another they are part of most people's constant preoccupation.

So, what with the shocking and the intimate element in the play, seeing it or reading it are unlikely to be negative experiences. You are likely to be touched or affected by it more or less violently, especially perhaps if you are passing through the same period of life as Alan. In some ways, it requires a strong stomach too. Apart from Alan's original 'crime', many later images and situations are disturbing, as Alan's experience is re-enacted in the psychiatrist's consulting-room; and if you are squeamish about cruelty to animals or embarrassed about teenage sexual fantasy, then you may well find the play difficult to approach in any detached critical way. You may experience it strongly without being able easily to write or talk about it. Shaffer might think that was a good thing, preferring that the audience should receive *Equus* as an experience in the theatre, and not an 'educational' exercise; yet the particular theatrical style of the play does invite the audience to remain in some ways detached.

In what ways is 'Equus' shocking? Have you found anything in 'Equus' embarassing? If so, what does that tell you about either yourself or the play?

Is 'theatre' literature?

Equus is essentially a piece of theatre, rather than a work of literature. This may seem to be a spurious distinction as any writing for the theatre must in some sense be literature, but Shaffer himself constantly stresses the equal importance of the visual action alongside the dialogue. This was especially true of *The Royal Hunt of the Sun*, Shaffer's first major achievement in 1964. In this play, about the conquest of the Peruvian Incas by the Spaniards in 1532, the visual effects are utterly essential to the experience of the play. The stage, in the original production, was dominated by a huge sun, which opened like the petals of a sunflower as the Conquistador, Pizarro, approached the city of the Inca King, Atahuallpa. Equally important were the strange and eerie musical effects created for this play, as for *Equus*, by the composer, Marc Wilkinson. If you see either of these plays for the first time in their later filmed versions, you will miss much of the original impact. The real sun, real mountains, and real horses do not necessarily have the same emotionally evocative effects as the emblems and symbols which appear in the stage productions. No real blood could ever have the same effect as the blood-cloth flowing out over the stage after the massacre of the Incas in *The Royal Hunt of the*

Sun. Similarly, no real gallop on a horse by a naked boy, in a film, will have the same intense concentration as the mimed gallop of Alan on Nugget at the centre of the spinning stage to the accompaniment of the sinister Equus Noise.

What does the reader of 'Equus' miss that the audience of the play in the theatre gains?

Is 'Equus' realistic?

These stage effects would be called non-naturalistic and are very much part of the style of the play. In the *Author's notes on the play* (page xxv), Shaffer points out that he had advice from a distinguished child psychiatrist. He adds, 'Through him I have tried to keep things real in a more naturalistic sense'. This must be taken to mean that the way in which the case is handled and indeed the whole framework of Alan's family background and situation are supposed to be fairly plausible, which seems to raise a big question about how we respond to the play. What is more important – the gradual emergence of Alan's 'real' experience as an isolated amalgam of sexual and religious images converted by the boy's loneliness into a fantasy of worship and passion, or the presentation of a case history in a working psychiatrist's general daily programme? If the former, we shall certainly feel that it is a theatrical experience which may move or disturb us and leave us reflecting about the nature of passion and worship. If the latter, we need to consider how important the psychiatric setting is.

Do you think of Alan as a 'case' or as a person?

Can you believe it?

In the same notes, Shaffer also points out that he came to perceive that psychiatrists are an 'immensely varied breed, professing varied methods and techniques'. It certainly doesn't seem to help much to consider what particular method or technique is being used by Martin Dysart, and what his method is based on. Clinical psychology is over a hundred years old now and it would be almost impossible to disentangle Dysart's particular professional ancestors. Nor is there any suggestion that he is at all special. He is an ordinary working psychiatrist, with a rather ordinary home, and rather ordinary tastes in the classics and Ancient Greece. The much bigger question which follows is how far Shaffer has succeeded in giving an impression of naturalism to the psychiatric investigation in a play which is quite obviously non-naturalistic. Some questions which point to an answer are: *How convincingly natural are most of the characters?* Martin and Alan are obviously studied in some depth, but what of the others? *How much do we believe in Frank and Dora Strang?* Are they not little more than types – lower middle-class with some pretentions to gentility, Dora dominated by old-fashioned religious fundamentalism, Frank by his doctrinaire socialism? Then, we might ask, *could such a serious mismatch occur?* Isn't the relation between Frank and Dora too sketchy if we are really to believe in the family pressures as a major source of Alan's disturbance? Dalton and the Young Horseman are even more obviously types, and Hesther and Jill not much fuller – though Hesther moves in the immediately 'real' world of Martin's consulting room (not merely in Alan's 'fictional' world), and Jill does offer some naturalistic explanation as to why she can't take Alan home when she says that her mother mistrusts men since her father ran off. But then, if you consider Frank, Dora, the Young Horseman, Dalton and Jill altogether you get a set of circumstances which are heavily stacked against Alan. The background to his condition is rather simplified. *Have we even been shown enough of Alan himself?* Why is he so isolated? Did he have no school friends? He doesn't seem to be the kind of boy who wouldn't mix at school, and who wouldn't get some of his private obsessions modified a bit by contact with others of his own age. Yet we see none of this side of his background, nor does Dysart ever enquire about it.

If you were studying Alan as a 'case' what more would you want to know about him than we are shown in the play?

In fact, the more closely we look, the more completely we see that the play is not really to be treated as a psychoanalytical casebook at all. To do so would be thoroughly misleading, and when Shaffer mentions his attempt to 'keep things real in a more naturalistic sense', he may be starting an unnecessary hare. The reason why all the characters, even including Alan, are rather limited and perhaps artificial is because the real subject of the play is Martin Dysart himself. With the sole and important exception of Hesther Salomon, all the other characters and experiences are conveyed to us as part of a narrative told by Martin, as past experience in Act One, and as present experience in Act Two. We receive everything therefore filtered through Martin's personality and present state of mind.

In your experience of the play, who is more central, Alan Strang or Martin Dysart?

When you consider the relationship between the powerful theatrical effect of the play and the somewhat sketchy characterisation it is not difficult to see why people have sometimes reacted against the play, seeing it as no more than a series of brilliant technical effects inadequately rooted in a compassionate and credible understanding of the characters who combine to make the effects.

If there is compassion in the play, it is most clearly seen for Martin Dysart. For him, the experience of Alan Strang is deeply disturbing. He is the character for whom at the end of the play we must feel pity. Alan Strang is undoubtedly deranged at the start, and we are to believe that he is equally undoubtedly cured at the end, once he has turned his suppressed memory into consciously accepted fact and transferred it to Dysart. It is perhaps a genuine weakness of the play that it is very difficult to contemplate seriously what Alan will become. Dysart's own interpretation of Alan's future is not very convincing. Would he really 'forget' quite so completely as is implied? However, that future, as Hesther clearly reminds us, is better for Alan than the pain of the past. It is Dysart who is left with the yawning gulf between the tedious actuality of daily life and the passionate engulfing possibilities that his imagination reveals – possibilities that in Alan he sees to have been brought into existence.

The key lies in Dysarts's opening speech which perhaps conveys more information than it should. How many members of an audience switch on to the real issues of a play in the first two or three minutes? (Shakespeare made the same mistake in *King Lear*!)

This opening speech makes quite clear the fact that this play is not a psychoanalytical case-book. Dysart is confronted with an extraordinary and totally confusing experience, which he plainly does not understand in terms of anything he is professionally familiar with. 'And of all the nonsensical things... what is the use of grief to a horse?...You see, I'm lost... they're worse than useless: they are, in fact, subversive...I'm desperate...a whole new track of being I only suspect is there...in a way, it has nothing to do with the boy...The extremity is the point...but intolerable.' These phrases convey Dysart's confusion, doubt, and sense of helplessness. And his commentaries on the progress of Alan's case and his own response to it, together with some of his conversations with Hesther, provide the focus through which we derive our 'understanding' of Alan's experience. It is what Alan means to him as a symbol of a more passionate type of existence than he has for himself or sees around him at present that matters, much more than Alan as a person in his own right; and seen like that the lack of fullness in Alan's character and background ceases to matter. Dysart sums up his dilemma at the end: 'I need – more desperately than my children need me – a way of seeing in the dark. What way is this? ... *What dark is this?*'

The ideal and the practical

In a Note on *Shrivings* (published in 1974), Shaffer writes:

> Man squeezed like a nut between an ideal choice and a practical one and cracked in bits by either is scarcely a novel image: yet the discovering of it for oneself, the coming to any sort of awareness of tragic ambiguity, must always be new and painful.

This, which is Dysart's discovery, has been the major preoccupation of Shaffer's most important plays, each of which is dominated by a pair of characters: Pizarro and Atahuallpa in *The Royal Hunt of the Sun* (1964), Mark Askelon and Gideon Petrie in *The Battle of Shrivings* (1970, rewritten as *Shrivings* in 1974 but not yet performed), Martin Dysart and Alan Strang in *Equus* (1973), and Salieri and Mozart in *Amadeus* (1979). In each case, one of the pair has qualities – very different in setting and circumstances but broadly related, visionary, inspirational, passionate, worshipful, spiritual, perhaps divine – which in the course of the play are (or appear to be) destroyed, leaving the other character in a state of despair or disillusionment. Pizarro wants to believe that Atahuallpa will come to life again when the sun rises at the end of *The Royal Hunt of the Sun*. Mark Askelon sets out to destroy the illusions of absolute pacifism held by Gideon Petrie but is appalled by the achievement of his aim, and by all his other destructions – his wife, his son, Petrie's secretary Lois. Dysart deeply regrets the loss of Alan's intense sexual and religious experience, even though he has caused that loss and all his reason said he should do so. Salieri, in the greatest of all these painful and ambiguous moments, cries at the end of *Amadeus* (the original version), 'If I cannot be Mozart, I do not wish to be anything.'

When we look at *Equus* in the light of Shaffer's other major works, we quickly see that the play is not, except incidentally, a picture of the psychoanalytic process, but an exploration – like all great plays – of the human condition, with all its confusions, paradoxes, and unanswerable questions. We are all likely to say 'I want life to be intense, passionate, exciting' as, in one sense, Alan's life – his secret life – has been. Equally, we are just as likely to share Hesther's view that Alan is in pain and if possible should be helped to resolve his crisis and return to the 'normal' world, however dull that may be. On the one hand, we can see Martin's personal distress as highly self-indulgent in a man with numerous advantages of position, possession and power. On the other, it may appear to us as a real and despairing awareness that what a man is can never quite match up to what he imagines he could be. Where you stand will determine what you think of the play. It is the writer's job to put the questions, not to provide the answers.

A note on the language

The language of the play is very carefully controlled to suggest economically the nature of the characters. The *Notes* on the text draw attention to a number of features in each character's mode of speech, which helps to bring them to life without the necessity of extensive description. Frank Strang's language is especially stereotyped, with its set phrases, 'Mind your own beeswax' and 'it's a *swiz*'. These and others quickly suggest his class awareness and desire to seem 'posher' than his position and job allow. Dora is much the same, while Hesther, Dalton and the Young Horseman are characterized as upper class, although Dalton and the Horseman are more obviously snobbish. Dysart himself is negative – his language has no distinguishing features, partly because he is the narrator, and partly because his career and the type of man he is would leave him largely without any definable class mannerisms. Alan's speech is very carefully judged especially in the calculated use of language only recently acceptable on the stage and in print. When he tells the nurse to 'fuck off', it has exactly the right weight of insolence. He knows he shouldn't say it, and his 'Do you fuck her?' to Dysart is even more carefully weighted. He knows it will cut, put like that without any euphemism. It is ironical that he is much less forthright once he is brought to the point when he speaks of his own experiences in that way.

A note on the author

Peter Shaffer was born in 1926 and lived in Liverpool until he was nine, when his parents moved to London. He went to the Hall School in Hampstead and then to St Paul's, from where he won an exhibition to Trinity College, Cambridge. Before that, however, he was called up – not for military service – but as a coal-miner, under the scheme brought in by Ernest Bevin, the then Minister of Labour and National Service. Conscripts of this type were known as 'Bevin boys'. He worked at Chislet colliery in Kent for two and a half years and then went up to Cambridge in 1947. At Cambridge he read history and, with his twin brother Anthony, edited the magazine *Granta*. From 1951–4 he worked at various jobs in New York, and wrote his first play, *The Salt Land*, while working in New York Public Library. The play was shown on ITV in 1955. When he returned to England he worked for the music publishers, Boosey and Hawkes, but resigned soon afterwards with the intention of devoting all his time to writing. During this period, he also published three novels written in collaboration with his brother and wrote another television play *Balance of Terror* – a spy thriller shown on BBC in 1957 – as well as a radio play, *The Prodigal Father* (also broadcast in 1957).

His first major success was *Five Finger Exercise*, performed at

the Comedy Theatre, London, in 1958, and from this time on
he saw himself as a playwright. The word itself is important to
him, especially the second syllable:

> I love that word playwright, particularly wright – it sug-
> gests a wheelwright or cartwright, a man with a hammer,
> hammering out a solid structure, and I've always tried to do
> that.

Equus

For Paul
with love

Author's note on the book

What appears in this book is a description of the first production of *Equus* at the National Theatre in July 1973. In making this description, I am partly satisfying myself, but also partly bowing to demand.

When people buy the published text of a new play, they mostly want to recall the experience they received in the theatre. That experience is composed, of course, not merely of the words they heard, but the gestures they saw, and the lighting, and the look of the thing.

There are, however, evils attendant on this sort of description. It can imprison a play in one particular stylization. Just as seriously, it can do a real injustice to the original Director, by incorporating his ideas without truly acknowledging them. Worse, if the Director is as inventive as John Dexter, it can actually seem to minimise those ideas, just by flatly setting down on paper what was far from flat on the stage, and listing inexpressively details of his work which, in accumulation, became deeply expressive.

Dexter directs powerfully through suggestion. Into the theatrical spaces he contrives, flows the communal imagination of an audience. He enables it to charge the action of a play with electric life. He is a master of gesture and of economy. Aesthetically, his founding fathers are Noh Drama and Bertholt Brecht: the plain plank; the clear light; the great pleasure in a set-piece. I do not mean by this that he would ever direct a single minute of physical action which detracted from the meaning of a play, or in some grand visual sense subverted it – he sharply dislikes effect isolated from context – but he is naturally and rightly drawn to plays which demand elaborate physical actions to complete them.

The Royal Hunt of the Sun and *Black Comedy*, both of which he directed, are such pieces: and so is *Equus*. Their visual action is to me as much a part of the play as the dialogue. I suppose my head has always been full of images. The gold masks staring hopefully and then in gathering despair at the sky, at the end of *The Royal Hunt of the Sun*, had been part of my imagination ever since I first saw a Peruvian funeral mask with its elongated eyes and red-smeared cheeks. Brindsley Miller in the lit-up darkness of *Black Comedy*, slowly moving the spiky legs of a Regency chair one inch before the innocent face of his spinster neighbour, had tiptoed that very journey in my head as I sat at my desk. But such images, like the Field of Ha Ha in *Equus* with its mist and nettles, still have to be externalized. In John Dexter's courageous and precise staging, they acquire a vibrant and unforgettable life.

While I am confessing debts, let me mention John Napier who created the tough, bright masks of horsedom; Andy Phillips who lit them superbly; and above all, Claude Chagrin, who animated them. She created, with the help of six human actors, a stable of Superhorses to stalk through the mind.

Finally, out of a fine company I must set down the names of three actors who made the first performance of this play live with a very special intensity. Alec McCowen's *Dysart* touched audiences deeply with its dry agony. Peter Firth's *Alan* left them sighing with admiration. Nicholas Clay's horse, *Nugget* was, quite simply, unforgettable.

Rehearsing a play is making the word flesh. Publishing a play is reversing the process. I can only hope this book is not too unjust to these brilliant people.

Author's notes on the play

One weekend over two years ago, I was driving with a friend through bleak countryside. We passed a stable. Suddenly he was reminded by it of an alarming crime which he had heard about recently at a dinner party in London. He knew only one horrible detail, and his complete mention of it could barely have lasted a minute – but it was enough to arouse in me an intense fascination.

The act had been committed several years before by a highly disturbed young man. It had deeply shocked a local bench of magistrates. It lacked, finally, any coherent explanation.

A few months later my friend died. I could not verify what he had said, or ask him to expand it. He had given me no name, no place, and no time. I don't think he knew them. All I possessed was his report of a dreadful event, and the feeling it engendered in me. I knew very strongly that I wanted to interpret it in some entirely personal way. I had to create a mental world in which the deed could be made comprehensible.

Every person and incident in *Equus* is of my own invention, save the crime itself: and even that I modified to accord with what I feel to be acceptable theatrical proportion. I am grateful now that I have never received confirmed details of the real story, since my concern has been more and more with a different kind of exploration.

I have been lucky, in doing final work on the play, to have enjoyed the advice and expert comment of a distinguished child psychiatrist. Through him I have tried to keep things real in a more naturalistic sense. I have also come to perceive that psychiatrists are an immensely varied breed, professing immensely varied methods and techniques. Martin Dysart is simply one doctor in one hospital. I must take responsibility for him, as I do for his patient.

The set

A square of wood set on a circle of wood.

The square resembles a railed boxing ring. The rail, also of wood, encloses three sides. It is perforated on each side by an opening. Under the rail are a few vertical slats, as if in a fence. On the downstage side there is no rail. The whole square is set on ball bearings, so that by slight pressure from actors standing round it on the circle, it can be made to turn round smoothly by hand.

On the square are set three little plain benches, also of wood. They are placed parallel with the rail, against the slats, but can be moved out by the actors to stand at right angles to them.

Set into the floor of the square, and flush with it, is a thin metal pole, about a yard high. This can be raised out of the floor, to stand upright. It acts as a support for the actor playing Nugget, when he is ridden.

In the area outside the circle stand benches. Two downstage left and right, are curved to accord with the circle. The left one is used by Dysart as a listening and observing post when he is out of the square, and also by Alan as his hospital bed. The right one is used by Alan's parents, who sit side by side on it. (Viewpoint is from the main body of the audience.)

Further benches stand upstage, and accommodate the other actors. All the cast of *Equus* sits on stage the entire evening. They get up to perform their scenes, and return when they are done to their places around the set. They are witnesses, assistants – and especially a Chorus.

Upstage, forming a backdrop to the whole, are tiers of seats in the fashion of a dissecting theatre, formed into two railed-off blocks, pierced by a central tunnel. In these blocks sit members of the audience. During the play, Dysart addresses them directly from time to time, as he addresses the main body of the theatre. No other actor ever refers to them.

To left and right, downstage, stand two ladders on which are suspended horse masks.

The colour of all benches is olive green.

Above the stage hangs a battery of lights, set in a huge metal ring. Light cues, in this version, will be only of the most general description.

The horses

The actors wear track-suits of chestnut velvet. On their feet are light strutted hooves, about four inches high, set on metal horse-shoes. On their hands are gloves of the same colour. On their heads are tough masks made of alternating bands of silver wire and leather: their eyes are outlined by leather blinkers. The actors' own heads are seen beneath them: no attempt should be made to conceal them.

Any literalism which could suggest the cosy familiarity of a domestic animal – or worse, a pantomime horse – should be avoided. The actors should never crouch on all fours, or even bend forward. They must always – except on the one occasion where Nugget is ridden – stand upright, as if the body of the horse extended invisibly behind them. Animal effect must be created entirely mimetically, through the use of legs, knees, neck, face, and the turn of the head which can move the mask above it through all the gestures of equine wariness and pride. Great care must also be taken that the masks are put on before the audience with very precise timing – the actors watching each other, so that the masking has an exact and ceremonial effect.

The Chorus

References are made in the text to the Equus Noise. I have in mind a choric effect, made by all the actors sitting round upstage, and composed of humming, thumping, and stamping – though never of neighing or whinnying. This Noise heralds or illustrates the presence of Equus the God.

Characters

MARTIN DYSART, *a psychiatrist*
ALAN STRANG
FRANK STRANG, *his father*
DORA STRANG, *his mother*
HESTHER SALOMON, *a magistrate*
JILL MASON
HARRY DALTON, *a stable owner*
A YOUNG HORSEMAN
A NURSE

Six actors – *including the Young Horseman, who also plays Nugget – appear as Horses.*

The main action of the play takes place in Rokeby Psychiatric Hospital in Southern England.

The time is the present.

The play is divided into numbered scenes, indicating a change of time or locale or mood. The action, however, is continuous.

Act One

1

Darkness.

Silence.

Dim light up on the square. In a spotlight stands Alan Strang, a lean boy of seventeen, in sweater and jeans. In front of him, the horse Nugget. Alan's pose represents a contour of great tenderness: his head is pressed against the shoulder of the horse, his hands stretching up to fondle its head. The horse in turn nuzzles his neck.

The flame of a cigarette lighter jumps in the dark. Lights come up slowly on the circle. On the left bench, downstage, Martin Dysart, smoking. A man in his mid-forties.

DYSART With one particular horse, called Nugget, he embraces. The animal digs its sweaty brow into his cheek, and they stand in the dark for an hour – like a necking couple. And of all nonsensical things – I keep thinking about the *horse*! Not the boy: the horse, and what it may be trying to do. I keep seeing that huge head kissing him with its chained mouth. Nudging through the metal some desire absolutely irrelevant to filling its belly or propagating its own kind. What desire could that be? Not to stay a horse any longer? Not to remain reined up for ever in those particular genetic strings? Is it possible, at certain moments we cannot imagine, a horse can add its sufferings together – the non-stop jerks and jabs that are its daily life – and turn them into grief? What use is grief to a horse?

Alan leads Nugget out of the square and they disappear together up the tunnel, the horse's hooves scraping delicately on the wood.

Dysart rises, and addresses both the large audience in the theatre and the smaller one on stage.

You see, I'm lost. What use, I should be asking, are questions like these to an overworked psychiatrist in a provincial

1

hospital? They're worse than useless: they are, in fact, sub-versive. *question his ability to self or cure.*

He enters the square. The light grows brighter.

The thing is, I'm desperate. You see, I'm wearing that horse's head myself. That's the feeling. All reined up in old language and old assumptions, straining to jump clean-hoofed on to a whole new track of being I only suspect is there. I can't see it, because my educated, average head is being held at the wrong angle. I can't jump because the bit forbids it, and my own basic force – my horsepower, if you like – is too little. The only thing I know for sure is this: a horse's head is finally unknowable to me. Yet I handle children's heads – which I must presume to be more compli-cated, at least in the area of my chief concern. ... In a way, it has nothing to do with this boy. The doubts have been there for years, piling up steadily in this dreary place. It's only the extremity of this case that's made them active. I know that. The *extremity* is the point! All the same, whatever the reason, they are now, these doubts, not just vaguely worry-ing – but intolerable ... I'm sorry. I'm not making much sense. Let me start properly: in order. It began one Monday last month, with Hesther's visit.

2

The light gets warmer.

He sits. Nurse enters the square.

the wise judge stands for reason

NURSE Mrs Salomon to see you, Doctor.

DYSART Show her in, please.

Nurse leaves and crosses to where Hesther sits.

Some days I blame Hesther. She brought him to me. But of course that's nonsense. What is he but a last straw? A last symbol? If it hadn't been him, it would have been the next patient, or the next. At least, I suppose so.

Hesther enters the square: a woman in her mid-forties.

HESTHER Hallo, Martin.

Dysart rises and kisses her on the cheek.

DYSART Madam Chairman! Welcome to the torture chamber!

HESTHER It's good of you to see me right away.

DYSART You're a welcome relief. Take a couch.

HESTHER It's been a day?

DYSART No – just a fifteen year old schizophrenic, and a girl of eight thrashed into catatonia by her father. Normal, really . . . You're in a state.

HESTHER Martin, this is the most shocking case I ever tried.

DYSART So you said on the phone.

HESTHER I mean it. My bench wanted to send the boy to prison. For life, if they could manage it. It took me two hours solid arguing to get him sent to you instead.

DYSART Me?

HESTHER I mean, to hospital.

DYSART Now look, Hesther. Before you say anything else, I can take no more patients at the moment. I can't even cope with the ones I have.

HESTHER You must.

DYSART Why?

HESTHER Because most people are going to be disgusted by the whole thing. Including doctors.

DYSART May I remind you I share this room with two highly competent psychiatrists?

HESTHER Bennett and Thoroughgood. They'll be as shocked as the public.

DYSART That's an absolutely unwarrantable statement.

HESTHER Oh, they'll be cool and exact. And underneath they'll be revolted, and immovably English. Just like my bench.

DYSART Well, what am I? Polynesian?

HESTHER You know exactly what I mean! . . . (*pause*) Please, Martin. It's vital. You're this boy's only chance.

DYSART Why? What's he done? Dosed some little girl's Pepsi

3

flippant exchange

with Spanish Fly? What could possibly throw your bench into two-hour convulsions?

HESTHER He blinded six horses with a metal spike.

A long pause.

DYSART Blinded?

HESTHER Yes.

DYSART All at once, or over a period?

HESTHER All on the same night.

DYSART Where?

HESTHER In a riding stable near Winchester. He worked there at weekends.

DYSART How old?

HESTHER Seventeen.

DYSART What did he say in Court?

HESTHER Nothing. He just sang.

DYSART Sang?

HESTHER Any time anyone asked him anything.

Pause.

Please take him, Martin. It's the last favour I'll ever ask you.

DYSART No, it's not.

HESTHER No, it's not – and he's probably abominable. All I know is, he needs you badly. Because there really is nobody within a hundred miles of your desk who can handle him. And perhaps understand what this is about. Also....

DYSART What?

HESTHER There's something very special about him.

DYSART In what way?

HESTHER Vibrations. *she is sensitive*

DYSART You and your vibrations.

HESTHER They're quite startling. You'll see.

DYSART When does he get here?

HESTHER Tomorrow morning. Luckily there was a bed in Neville Ward. I know this is an awful imposition, Martin. Frankly I didn't know what else to do.

Pause.

DYSART Can you come in and see me on Friday?

HESTHER Bless you!

DYSART If you come after work I can give you a drink. Will 6.30 be all right?

HESTHER You're a dear. You really are.

DYSART Famous for it.

HESTHER Goodbye.

DYSART By the way, what's his name?

HESTHER Alan Strang.

She leaves and returns to her seat.

DYSART (*to audience*) What did I expect of him? Very little, I promise you. One more dented little face. One more adolescent freak. The usual unusual. One great thing about being in the adjustment business: you're never short of customers.

Nurse comes down the tunnel, followed by Alan. She enters the square.

NURSE Alan Strang, Doctor.

The boy comes in.

DYSART Hallo. My name's Martin Dysart. I'm pleased to meet you.

He puts out his hand. Alan does not respond in any way.

That'll be all, Nurse, thank you.

3

Nurse goes out and back to her place. Dysart sits, opening a file.

So: did you have a good journey? I hope they gave you lunch at least. Not that there's much to choose between a British Rail meal and one here.

Alan stands staring at him.

DYSART Won't you sit down?

Pause. He does not. Dysart consults his file.

Is this your full name? Alan Strang?

Silence.

And you're seventeen. Is that right? Seventeen? . . . Well?

ALAN (*singing low*) Double your pleasure
  Double your fun
  With Doublemint, Doublemint
  Doublemint gum.

DYSART (*unperturbed*) Now, let's see. You work in an electrical
  shop during the week. You live with your parents, and your
  father's a printer. What sort of things does he print?

ALAN (*singing louder*) Double your pleasure
  Double your fun
  With Doublemint, Doublemint
  Doublemint gum.

DYSART I mean does he do leaflets and calendars? Things like
  that?

The boy approaches him, hostile.

ALAN (*singing*) Try the taste of Martini
  The most beautiful drink in the world.
  It's the right one –
  The bright one –
  That's Martini!

DYSART I wish you'd sit down, if you're going to sing. Don't
  you think you'd be more comfortable?

Pause.

ALAN (*singing*) There's only one T in Typhoo!
  In packets and in teabags too.
  Any way you make it, you'll find it's true:
  There's only one T in Typhoo!

DYSART (*appreciatively*) Now that's a good song. I like it better
  than the other two. Can I hear that one again?

Alan starts away from him, and sits on the upstage bench.

ALAN (*singing*) Double your pleasure
  Double your fun
  With Doublemint, Doublemint
  Doublemint gum.

DYSART (*smiling*) You know I was wrong. I really do think that
  one's better. It's got such a catchy tune. Please do that one
  again.

Silence. The boy glares at him.

   I'm going to put you in a private bedroom for a little while.
There are one or two available, and they're rather more
pleasant than being in a ward. Will you please come and see
me tomorrow? ... (*He rises*) By the way, which parent is it
who won't allow you to watch television? Mother or father?
Or is it both? (*calling out of the door*) Nurse!
Alan stares at him. Nurse comes in.

NURSE Yes, Doctor?

DYSART Take Strang here to Number Three, will you? He's
moving in there for a while.

NURSE Very good, Doctor.

DYSART (*to Alan*) You'll like that room. It's nice.

The boy sits staring at Dysart. Dysart returns the stare.

NURSE Come along, young man. This way. ... I said this way,
please.

*Reluctantly Alan rises and goes to Nurse, passing dangerously close to
Dysart, and out through the left door. Dysart looks after him, fascinated.*

4

*Nurse and patient move on to the circle, and walk downstage to the bench
where the doctor first sat, which is to serve also as Alan's bed.*

NURSE Well now: isn't this nice? You're lucky to be in here,
you know, rather than the ward. That ward's a noisy old
place.

ALAN (*singing*) Let's go where you wanna go – Texaco!

NURSE (*contemplating him*) I hope you're not going to make a
nuisance of yourself. You'll have a much better time of it
here, you know, if you behave yourself.

ALAN Fuck off.

NURSE (*tight*) That's the bell there. The lav's down the corri-
dor.

She leaves him, and goes back to her place. Alan lies down.

5

Dysart stands in the middle of the square and addresses the audience. He is agitated.

DYSART That night, I had this very explicit dream. In it I'm a chief priest in Homeric Greece. I'm wearing a wide gold mask, all noble and bearded, like the so-called Mask of Agamemnon found at Mycenae. I'm standing by a thick round stone and holding a sharp knife. In fact, I'm officiating at some immensely important ritual sacrifice, on which depends the fate of the crops or of a military expedition. The sacrifice is a herd of children: about five hundred boys and girls. I can see them stretching away in a long queue, right across the plain of Argos. I know it's Argos because of the red soil. On either side of me stand two assistant priests, wearing masks as well: lumpy, pop-eyed masks, such as also were found at Mycenae. They are enormously strong, these other priests, and absolutely tireless. As each child steps forward, they grab it from behind and throw it over the stone. Then, with a surgical skill which amazes even me, I fit in the knife and slice elegantly down to the navel, just like a seamstress following a pattern. I part the flaps, sever the inner tubes, yank them out and throw them hot and steaming on to the floor. The other two then study the pattern they make, as if they were reading hieroglyphics. It's obvious to me that I'm tops as chief priest. It's this unique talent for carving that has got me where I am. The only thing is, unknown to them, I've started to feel distinctly nauseous. And with each victim, it's getting worse. My face is going green behind the mask. Of course, I redouble my efforts to look professional – cutting and snipping for all I'm worth: mainly because I know that if ever those two assistants so much as glimpse my distress – and the implied doubt that this repetitive and smelly work is doing any social good at all – I will be the next across the stone. And

8

then, of course – the damn mask begins to slip. The priests both turn and look at it – it slips some more – they see the green sweat running down my face – their gold pop-eyes suddenly fill up with blood – they tear the knife out of my hand . . . and I wake up.

6

Hesther enters the square. Light grows warmer.

HESTHER That's the most indulgent thing I ever heard.

DYSART You think?

HESTHER Please don't be ridiculous. You've done the most su-perb work with children. You must know that.

DYSART Yes, but do the children?

HESTHER Really!

DYSART I'm sorry.

HESTHER So you should be.

DYSART I don't know why you listen. It's just professional menopause. Everyone gets it sooner or later. Except you.

HESTHER Oh, of course. I feel totally fit to be a magistrate all the time. *Sarcasm*

DYSART No, you don't – but then that's you feeling <u>unworthy</u> <u>to fill a job</u>. I feel the job is unworthy to fill me.

HESTHER Do you seriously?

DYSART More and more. I'd like to spend the next ten years wandering very slowly around the *real* Greece . . . Anyway, all this dream nonsense is your fault.

HESTHER Mine?

DYSART It's that lad of yours who started it off. Do you know it's his face I saw on every victim across the stone?

HESTHER Strang?

DYSART He has the strangest stare I ever met.

HESTHER Yes.

DYSART <u>It's exactly like being accused. Violently accused.</u> But

9

what of?... Treating him is going to be unsettling. Especially in my present state. His singing was direct enough. His speech is more so.

HESTHER (*surprised*) He's talking to you, then?

DYSART Oh yes. It took him two more days of commercials, and then he snapped. Just like that – I suspect it has something to do with his nightmares.

Nurse walks briskly round the circle, a blanket over her arm, a clipboard of notes in her hand.

HESTHER He has nightmares?

DYSART Bad ones.

NURSE We had to give him a sedative or two, Doctor. Last night it was exactly the same.

DYSART (*to Nurse*) What does he do? Call out?

NURSE (*to desk*) A lot of screaming, Doctor.

DYSART (*to Nurse*) Screaming?

NURSE One word in particular.

DYSART (*to Nurse*) You mean a special word?

NURSE Over and over again. (*consulting clipboard*) It sounds like 'Ek'.

HESTHER Ek?

NURSE Yes, Doctor. Ek... 'Ek!' he goes. 'Ek!'

HESTER How weird.

NURSE When I woke him up he clung to me like he was going to break my arm.

She stops at Alan's bed. He is sitting up. She puts the blanket over him, and returns to her place.

DYSART And then he burst in – just like that – without knocking or anything. Fortunately, I didn't have a patient with me.

ALAN (*jumping up*) Dad!

HESTHER What?

DYSART The answer to a question I'd asked him two days before. Spat out with the same anger as he sang the commercials.

HESTHER Dad what?

10

ALAN Who hates telly.

He lies downstage on the circle, as if watching television.

HESTHER You mean his dad forbids him to watch?

DYSART Yes.

ALAN It's a dangerous drug.

HESTHER Oh, really!

Frank stands up and enters the scene downstage on the circle. A man in his fifties.

FRANK (*to Alan*) It may not look like that, but that's what it is. Absolutely fatal mentally, if you receive my meaning.

Dora follows him on. She is also middle-aged.

DORA That's a little extreme, dear, isn't it?

FRANK You sit in front of that thing long enough, you'll become stupid for life – like most of the population. (*to Alan*) The thing is, it's a *swiz*. It seems to be offering you something, but actually it's taking something away. Your intelligence and your concentration, every minute you watch it. That's a true swiz, do you see?

Seated on the floor, Alan shrugs.

I don't want to sound like a spoilsport, old chum – but there really is no substitute for reading. What's the matter: don't you like it?

ALAN It's all right.

FRANK I know you think it's none of my beeswax, but it really is you know ... Actually, it's a disgrace when you come to think of it. You the son of a printer, and never opening a book! If all the world was like you, I'd be out of a job, if you receive my meaning! *Reading equaled to keeping a job*

DORA All the same, times change, Frank.

FRANK (*reasonably*) They change if you let them change, Dora. Please return that set in the morning.

ALAN (*crying out*) No!

DORA Frank! No!

FRANK I'm sorry, Dora, but I'm not having that thing in the house a moment longer. I told you I didn't want it to begin with.

11

DORA But, dear, everyone watches television these days!

FRANK Yes, and what do they watch? <u>Mindless</u> violence! <u>Mindless</u> jokes! Every five minutes some laughing idiot selling you something you don't want, just to <u>bolster</u> up the <u>economic system</u>. (*to Alan*) I'm sorry, old chum.

He leaves the scene and sits again in his place.

HESTHER He's a Communist, then?

DYSART Old-type Socialist, I'd say. Relentlessly self-improving.

HESTHER They're *both* older than you'd expect.

DYSART So I gather.

DORA (*looking after Frank*) Really, dear, you are very extreme!

She leaves the scene too, and again sits beside her husband.

HESTHER She's an ex-school teacher, isn't she?

DYSART Yes. The boy's proud of that. We got on to it this afternoon.

ALAN (*belligerently, standing up*) She knows more than you.

Hesther crosses and sits by Dysart. During the following, the boy walks round the circle, speaking to Dysart but not looking at him. Dysart replies in the same manner.

DYSART (*to Alan*) Does she?

ALAN I bet I do too. I bet I know more history than you.

DYSART (*to Alan*) Well, I bet you don't.

ALAN All right: who was the Hammer of the Scots?

DYSART (*to Alan*) I don't know: who?

ALAN <u>King</u> Edward the First. Who never smiled again?

DYSART (*to Alan*) I don't know: who?

ALAN You don't know anything, do you? It was Henry the First. I know all the <u>Kings</u>.

DYSART (*to Alan*) And who's your favourite?

ALAN John.

DYSART (*to Alan*) Why?

ALAN Because he <u>put out the eyes</u> of that smarty little –

Pause.

(*sensing he has said something wrong*) Well, he didn't really. He was prevented, because the gaoler was merciful!

HESTHER Oh dear.

ALAN *He was prevented!*

DYSART Something odder was to follow.

ALAN Who said 'Religion is the opium of the people'?

HESTHER Good Lord!

Alan giggles.

DYSART The odd thing was, he said it with a sort of guilty snigger. The sentence is obviously associated with some kind of tension.

HESTHER What did you say?

DYSART I gave him the right answer. (*to Alan*) Karl Marx.

ALAN No.

DYSART (*to Alan*) Then who?

ALAN Mind your own beeswax

DYSART It's probably his dad. He may say it to provoke his wife.

HESTHER And you mean she's religious?

DYSART She could be. I tried to discover – none too success-fully.

ALAN Mind your own beeswax!

Alan goes back to bed and lies down in the dark.

DYSART However, I shall find out on Sunday.

HESTHER What do you mean?

DYSART (*getting up*) I want to have a look at his home, so I invited myself over.

HESTHER Did you?

DYSART If there's any tension over religion, it should be evident on a Sabbath evening! I'll let you know.

He kisses her cheek and they part, both leaving the square. Hesther sits in her place again; Dysart walks round the circle, and greets Dora who stands waiting for him downstage.

7

DYSART (*shaking hands*) Mrs Strang.

13

DORA Mr Strang's still at the Press, I'm afraid. He should be home in a minute.

DYSART He works Sundays as well?

DORA Oh, yes. He doesn't set much store by Sundays.

DYSART Perhaps you and I could have a little talk before he comes in.

DORA Certainly. Won't you come into the living room?

She leads the way into the square. She is very nervous.

Please . . . .

She motions him to sit, then holds her hands tightly together.

DYSART Mrs Strang, have you any idea how this thing could have occurred?

DORA I can't imagine, Doctor. It's all so unbelievable! . . . Alan's always been such a gentle boy. He loves animals! Especially horses.

DYSART Especially?

DORA Yes. He even has a photograph of one up in his bedroom. A beautiful white one, looking over a gate. His father gave it to him a few years ago, off a calendar he'd printed – and he's never taken it down . . . And when he was seven or eight, I used to have to read him the same book over and over, all *about* a horse.

DYSART Really?

DORA Yes: it was called Prince, and no one could ride him.

Alan calls from his bed, not looking at his mother.

ALAN (*excited, younger voice*) Why not? . . . Why not? . . . Say it! In his voice!

DARA He loved the idea of animals talking.

DYSART Did he?

ALAN *Say it! Say it! . . . Use his voice!*

DORA (*'proud' voice*) 'Because I am faithful!'

Alan giggles.

'My name is Prince, and I'm a Prince among horses! Only my young Master can ride me! Anyone else – I'll *throw off!*'

Alan giggles louder.

And then I remember I used to tell him a funny thing about

falling off horses. Did you know that when Christian cavalry first appeared in the New World, the <u>pagans thought <u>horse</u> and rider was one person?</u>

DYSART Really?

ALAN (*sitting up, amazed*) One person?

DORA Actually, they thought it must be a <u>god.</u>

ALAN *A god!*

DORA It was only when one rider fell off, they realized the truth.

DYSART That's fascinating. I never heard that before. . . . Can you remember anything else like that you may have told him about horses?

DORA Well, not really. They're in the Bible, of course. 'He saith among the trumpets, Ha, ha.'

DYSART Ha, ha?

DORA The Book of Job. Such a noble passage. *You* know — (*quoting*) 'Hast thou given the horse strength?'

ALAN (*responding*) 'Hast thou clothed his neck with thunder?'

DORA (*to Alan*) 'The glory of his nostrils is terrible!'

ALAN 'He swallows the ground with fierceness and rage!'

DORA 'He saith among the trumpets —'

ALAN (*trumpeting*) 'Ha! Ha!'

DORA (*to Dysart*) Isn't that splendid?

DYSART It certainly is.

ALAN (*trumpeting*) Ha! Ha!

DORA And then, of course, we saw an awful lot of Westerns on the television. He couldn't have enough of those.

DYSART But surely you don't have a set, do you? I understood Mr Strang doesn't approve.

DORA (*conspiratorially*) He doesn't . . . I used to let him slip off in the afternoons to a friend next door.

DYSART (*smiling*) You mean without his father's knowledge?

DORA What the eye does not see, the heart does not grieve over, does it? Anyway, Westerns are harmless enough, surely?

Frank stands up and enters the square. Alan lies back under the blanket.

15

(*to Frank*) Oh, hallo dear. This is Dr Dysart.

FRANK (*shaking hands*) How d'you do?

DYSART How d'you do?

DORA I was just telling the Doctor, Alan's always adored horses.

FRANK (*tight*) We assumed he did.

DORA You know he did, dear. Look how he liked that photograph you gave him.

FRANK (*startled*) What about it?

DORA Nothing dear. Just that he pestered you to have it as soon as he saw it. Do you remember? (*to Dysart*) We've always been a horsey family. At least my side of it has. My grandfather used to ride every morning on the downs behind Brighton, all dressed up in bowler hat and jodhpurs! He used to look splendid. Indulging in equitation, he called it.

Frank moves away from them and sits wearily.

ALAN (*trying the word*) <u>Equitation</u>....

DORA I remember I told him how that came from *equus*, the Latin word for horse. Alan was fascinated by that word, I know. I suppose because he'd never come across one with two U's together before.

ALAN (*savouring it*) *Equus!*

DORA I always wanted the boy to ride himself. He'd have so enjoyed it.

DYSART But surely he did?

DORA No.

DYSART Never?

DORA He didn't care for it. He was most definite about not wanting to.

DYSART But he must have had to at the stables? I mean, it would be part of the job.

DORA You'd have thought so, but no. He absolutely wouldn't, would he, dear?

FRANK (*dryly*) It seems he was perfectly happy raking out manure.

DYSART Did he ever give a reason for this?

16

DORA No. I must say we both thought it most peculiar, but he wouldn't discuss it. I mean, you'd have thought he'd be longing to get out in the air after being cooped up all week in that dreadful shop. Electrical and kitchenware! Isn't *that* an environment for a sensitive boy, Doctor?...

FRANK Dear, have you offered the doctor a cup of tea?

DORA Oh dear, no, I haven't!... And you must be dying for one.

DYSART That would be nice.

DORA Of course it would... Excuse me...

She goes out – but lingers on the circle, eavesdropping near the right door. Alan stretches out under his blanket and sleeps. Frank gets up.

FRANK My wife has romantic ideas, if you receive my meaning.

DYSART About her family?

FRANK She thinks she married beneath her. I daresay she did. I don't understand these things myself.

DYSART Mr Strang, I'm fascinated by the fact that Alan wouldn't ride.

FRANK Yes, well that's him. He's always been a weird lad, I have to be honest. Can you imagine spending your weekends like that – just cleaning out stalls – with all the things that he could have been doing in the way of Further Education?

DYSART Except he's hardly a scholar.

FRANK How do we know? He's never really tried. His mother indulged him. She doesn't care if he can hardly write his own name, and she a school teacher that was. Just as long as he's happy, she says...

Dora wrings her hands in anguish. Frank sits again.

DYSART Would you say she was closer to him than you are?

FRANK They've always been thick as thieves. I can't say I entirely approve – especially when I hear her whispering that Bible to him hour after hour, up there in his room.

DYSART Your wife is religious?

FRANK Some might say excessively so. Mind you, that's her business. But when it comes to dosing it down the boy's throat – well, frankly, he's my son as well as hers. She

17

doesn't see that. Of course, that's the funny thing about religious people. They always think their susceptibilities are more important than non-religious.

DYSART And you're non-religious, I take it?

FRANK I'm an atheist, and I don't mind admitting it. If you want my opinion, it's the Bible that's responsible for all this.

DYSART Why?

FRANK Well, look at it yourself. A boy spends night after night having this stuff read into him: an innocent man tortured to death – thorns driven into his head – nails into his hands – a spear jammed through his ribs. It can mark anyone for life, that kind of thing. I'm not joking. The boy was absolutely fascinated by all that. He was always mooning over religious pictures. I mean real kinky ones, if you receive my meaning. I had to put a stop to it once or twice! ... (*pause*) Bloody religion – it's our only real problem in this house, but it's insuperable: I don't mind admitting it.

Unable to stand any more, Dora comes in again.

DORA (*pleasantly*) You must excuse my husband, Doctor. This one subject is something of an obsession with him, isn't it, dear? You must admit.

FRANK Call it what you like. All that stuff to me is just bad sex.

DORA And what has that got to do with Alan?

FRANK Everything! ... (*seriously*) Everything, Dora!

DORA I don't understand. What are you saying?

He turns away from her.

DYSART (*calmingly*) Mr Strang, exactly how informed do you judge your son to *be* about sex?

FRANK (*tight*) I don't know.

DYSART You didn't actually instruct him yourself?

FRANK Not in so many words, no.

DYSART Did *you*, Mrs Strang?

DORA Well, I spoke a little, yes. I had to. I've been a teacher, Doctor, and I know what happens if you don't. They find out through magazines and dirty books.

DYSART What sort of thing did you tell him? I'm sorry if this is embarrassing.

DORA I told him the biological facts. But I also told him what I believed. That sex is not *just* a biological matter, but spiritual as well. That if God willed, he would fall in love one day. That his task was to prepare himself for the most important happening of his life. And after that, if he was lucky, he might come to know a higher love still ... I simply ... don't understand.... *Alan!* ...

She breaks down in sobs. Her husband gets up and goes to her.

FRANK (*embarrassed*) There now. There now, Dora. Come on!

DORA (*with sudden desperation*) All right – laugh! Laugh, as usual!

FRANK (*kindly*) No one's laughing, Dora.

She glares at him. He puts his arms round her shoulders.

No one's laughing, are they Doctor?

Tenderly, he leads his wife out of the square, and they resume their places on the bench.

Lights grow much dimmer.

8

A strange noise begins. Alan begins to murmur from his bed. He is having a bad nightmare, moving his hands and body as if frantically straining to tug something back. Dysart leaves the square as the boy's cries increase.

ALAN Ek! ... Ek! ... *Ek!* ...

Cries of Ek! *on tape fill the theatre, from all around. Dysart reaches the foot of Alan's bed as the boy gives a terrible cry —*

EK!

— and wakes up. The sounds snap off. Alan and the Doctor stare at each other. Then abruptly Dysart leaves the area and re-enters the square.

9

Lights grow brighter.

Dysart sits on his bench, left, and opens his file. Alan gets out of bed, leaves his blanket, and comes in. He looks truculent.

DYSART Hallo. How are you this morning?

Alan stares at him.

Come on: sit down.

Alan crosses the stage and sits on the bench, opposite.

Sorry if I gave you a start last night. I was collecting some papers from my office, and I thought I'd look in on you. Do you dream often?

ALAN Do *you?*

DYSART It's my job to ask the questions. Yours to answer them.

ALAN Says who?

DYSART Says me. Do you dream often?

ALAN Do you?

DYSART Look – Alan.

ALAN I'll answer if you answer. In turns.

Pause.

DYSART Very well. Only we have to speak the truth.

ALAN (*mocking*) Very well.

DYSART So. Do you dream often?

ALAN Yes. Do you?

DYSART Yes. Do you have a special dream?

ALAN No. Do you?

DYSART Yes. What was your dream about last night?

ALAN Can't remember. What's yours about?

DYSART I said the truth.

ALAN That is the truth. What's yours about? The special one.

DYSART Carving up children.

Alan smiles.

My turn!

ALAN What?

20

DYSART What is your first memory of a horse?

ALAN What d'you mean?

DYSART The first time one entered your life, in any way.

ALAN Can't remember.

DYSART Are you sure?

ALAN Yes.

DYSART You have no recollection of the first time you noticed
a horse?

ALAN I told you. Now it's my turn. Are you married?

DYSART (*controlling himself*) I am.

ALAN Is she a doctor too?

DYSART It's my turn.

ALAN Yes, well what?

DYSART What is Ek?

Pause.

You shouted it out last night in your sleep. I thought you
might like to talk about it.

ALAN (*singing*) Double Diamond works wonders,

Works wonders, works wonders!

DYSART Come on, now. You can do better than that.

ALAN (*singing louder*) Double Diamond works wonders,

Works wonders

For you!

DYSART All right. Good morning.

ALAN What d'you mean?

DYSART We're finished for today.

ALAN But I've only had ten minutes.

DYSART Too bad.

He picks up a file and studies it. Alan lingers.

Didn't you hear me? I said, Good morning.

ALAN That's not fair!

DYSART No?

ALAN (*savagely*) The Government pays you twenty quid an
hour to see me. I know. I heard downstairs.

DYSART Well, go back there and hear some more.

ALAN *That's not fair!*

21

He springs up clenching his fists in a sudden violent rage.

You're a – you're a – You're a swiz!...Bloody swiz!...
Fucking swiz! *The conflict between the members of the family.*

DYSART Do I have to call Nurse?

ALAN She puts a finger on me, I'll bash her!

DYSART She'll bash you much harder, I can assure you. Now go away.

He reads his file. Alan stays where he is, emptily clenching his hands. He turns away.

A pause.

A faint hum starts from the Chorus.

ALAN (*sullenly*) On a beach. ...

10

He steps out of the square, upstage, and begins to walk round the circle. Warm light glows on it.

DYSART What?

ALAN Where I saw a horse. Swizzy.

Lazily he kicks at the sand, and throws stones at the sea.

DYSART How old were you?

ALAN How should I know? ... Six.

DYSART Well, go on. What were you doing there?

ALAN Digging.

He throws himself on the ground, downstage centre of the circle, and starts scuffing with his hands.

DYSART A sandcastle?

ALAN Well, what else?

DYSART (*warningly*) And?

ALAN Suddenly I heard this noise. Coming up behind me.

A young Horseman issues in slow motion out of the tunnel. He carries a riding crop with which he is urging on his invisible horse, down the right side of the circle.

The hum increases.

DYSART What noise?

ALAN Hooves. Splashing.

DYSART Splashing?

ALAN The tide was out and he was galloping.

DYSART Who was?

ALAN This fellow. Like a college chap. He was on a big horse
– urging him on. I thought he hadn't seen me. I called out:
Hey!

The horseman goes into natural time, *charging fast round the downstage corner of the square straight at Alan.*

and they just swerved in time!

HORSEMAN (*reining back*) Whoa!...Whoa there! *Whoa!*...
Sorry! I didn't see you!...Did I scare you?

ALAN No!

HORSEMAN (*looking down on him*) That's a terrific castle!

ALAN What's his name?

HORSEMAN Trojan. You can stroke him, if you like. He won't
mind.

Shyly Alan stretches up on tip-toe, and pats an invisible shoulder.

(*amused*) You can hardly reach down there. Would you like
to come up?

Alan nods, eyes wide.

All right. Come round this side. You always mount a horse
from the left. I'll give you a lift. O.K.?

Alan goes round on the other side.

Here we go, now. Just do nothing. Upsadaisy!

*Alan set his foot on the Horseman's thigh, and is lifted by him up on to
his shoulders.*

The hum from the Chorus becomes exultant. Then stops.

All right?

Alan nods.

Good. Now all you do is hold onto his mane.

He holds up the crop, and Alan grips on to it.

Tight now. And grip with your knees. All right?

All set? ... Come on, then, Trojan. Let's go!

The Horseman walks slowly upstage round the circle, with Alan's legs tight round his neck.

DYSART How was it? Was it wonderful?

Alan rides in silence.

Can't you remember?

HORSEMAN Do you want to go faster?

ALAN Yes!

HORSEMAN O.K. All you have to do is say 'Come on, Trojan – bear me away!' . . . Say it, then!

ALAN Bear me away!

The Horesman starts to run with Alan round the circle.

DYSART You went fast?

ALAN Yes!

DYSART Weren't you frightened?

ALAN No!

HORSEMAN Come on now, Trojan! Bear us away! Hold on! Come on now! . . .

He runs faster. Alan begins to laugh. Then suddenly, as they reach again the right downstage corner, Frank and Dora stand up in alarm.

DORA Alan!

FRANK Alan!

DORA Alan, stop!

Frank runs round after them. Dora follows behind.

FRANK Hey, you! *You!* . . .

HORSEMAN Whoa, boy! . . . Whoa! . . .

He reins the horse round, and wheels to face the parents. This all goes fast.

FRANK What do you imagine you are doing?

HORSEMAN (*ironic*) 'Imagine'?

FRANK What is my son doing up there?

HORSEMAN Water-skiing!

Dora joins them, breathless.

DORA Is he all right, Frank? . . . He's not hurt?

FRANK Don't you think you should ask permission before doing a stupid thing like that?

HORSEMAN What's stupid?

ALAN It's lovely, dad!

DORA Alan, come down here!

HORSEMAN The boy's perfectly safe. Please don't be hysterical.

FRANK Don't you be la-di-da with me, young man! Come down here, Alan. You heard what your mother said.

ALAN No.

FRANK Come down at once. Right this moment.

ALAN No. ... NO!

FRANK (*in a fury*) I said – this moment!

He pulls Alan from the Horseman's shoulders. The boy shrieks, and falls to the ground.

HORSEMAN Watch it!

DORA Frank!

She runs to her son, and kneels. The Horseman skitters.

HORSEMAN Are you mad? D'you want to terrify the horse?

DORA He's grazed his knee. Frank – the boy's hurt!

ALAN I'm not! I'm *not!*

FRANK What's your name?

HORSEMAN Jesse James.

DORA Frank, he's bleeding!

FRANK I intend to report you to the police for endangering the lives of children.

HORSEMAN Go right ahead!

DORA Can you stand, dear?

ALAN Oh, *stop* it! ...

FRANK You're a public menace, d'you know that? How dare you pick up children and put them on dangerous animals.

HORSEMAN Dangerous?

FRANK Of course dangerous. Look at his eyes. They're rolling.

HORSEMAN So are yours!

FRANK In my opinion that is a dangerous animal. In my considered opinion you are both dangers to the safety of this beach.

HORSEMAN And in my opinion, you're a stupid fart!

DORA Frank, leave it!

FRANK What did you say?

DORA It's not important, Frank – really!

25

FRANK *What did you say?*

HORSEMAN Oh bugger off! Sorry, chum! Come on, Trojan!

He urges his horse straight at them, then wheels it and gallops off round the right side of the circle and away up the tunnel, out of sight. The parents cry out, as they are covered with sand and water. Frank runs after him, and round the left side of the circle, with his wife following after.

ALAN Splash, splash, splash! All three of us got covered with water! Dad got absolutely soaked!

FRANK (*shouting after the Horseman*) Hooligan! Filthy hooligan!

ALAN I wanted to laugh!

FRANK Upper class riff-raff! That's all they are, people who go riding! That's what they *want* – trample on ordinary people!

DORA Don't be absurd, Frank.

FRANK It's why they do it. It's why they bloody do it!

DORA (*amused*) Look at you. You're covered!

FRANK Not as much as you. There's sand all over your hair!

She starts to laugh.

(*shouting*) Hooligan! Bloody hooligan!

She starts to laugh more. He tries to brush the sand out of her hair.

What are you laughing at? It's not funny. It's not funny at all, Dora!

She goes off, right, still laughing. Alan edges into the square, still on the ground.

It's just not funny! . . .

Frank returns to his place on the beach, sulky.

Abrupt silence.

ALAN And that's all I remember.

DYSART And a lot, too. Thank you . . . You know, I've never been on a horse in my life.

ALAN (*not looking at him*) Nor me.

DYSART You mean, after that?

ALAN Yes.

DYSART But you must have done at the stables?

ALAN No.

DYSART Never?

ALAN No.

DYSART How come?

ALAN I didn't care to.

DYSART Did it have anything to do with falling off like that, all those years ago?

ALAN (*tight*) I just didn't care to, that's all.

DYSART Do you think of that scene often?

ALAN I suppose.

DYSART Why, do you think?

ALAN 'Cos it's funny.

DYSART Is that all?

ALAN What else? My turn.... I told you a secret: now you tell me one.

DYSART All right. I have patients who've got things to tell me, only they're ashamed to say them to my face. What do you think I do about that?

ALAN What?

DYSART I give them this little tape recorder.

He takes a small tape recorder and microphone from his pocket.

They go off to another room, and send me the tape through Nurse. They don't have to listen to it with me.

ALAN That's stupid.

DYSART All you do is press this button, and speak into this. It's very simple. Anyway, your time's up for today. I'll see you tomorrow.

ALAN (*getting up*) Maybe.

DYSART Maybe?

ALAN If I feel like it.

He is about to go out. Then suddenly he returns to Dysart and takes the machine from him.

It's stupid.

He leaves the square and goes back to his bed.

27

11

DORA (*calling out*) Doctor!

Dora re-enters and comes straight on to the square from the right. She wears an overcoat, and is nervously carrying a shopping bag.

DYSART That same evening, his mother appeared.

DORA Hallo, Doctor.

DYSART Mrs Strang!

DORA I've been shopping in the neighbourhood. I thought I might just look in.

DYSART Did you want to see Alan?

DORA (*uncomfortably*) No, no...Not just at the moment. Actually, it's more you I wanted to see.

DYSART Yes?

DORA You see, there's something Mr Strang and I thought you ought to know. We discussed it, and it might just be important.

DYSART Well, come and sit down.

DORA I can't stay more than a moment. I'm late as it is. Mr Strang will be wanting his dinner.

DYSART Ah. (*encouragingly*) So, what was it you wanted to tell me?

She sits on the upstage bench.

DORA Well, do you remember that photograph I mentioned to you. The one Mr Strang gave Alan to decorate his bedroom a few years ago?

DYSART Yes. A horse looking over a gate, wasn't it?

DORA That's right. Well, actually, it took the place of another kind of picture altogether.

DYSART What kind?

DORA It was a reproduction of Our Lord on his way to Calvary. Alan found it in Reeds Art Shop, and fell absolutely in love with it. He insisted on buying it with his pocket money, and hanging it at the foot of his bed where he could see it last thing at night. My husband was very displeased.

DYSART Because it was religious?

DORA In all fairness I must admit it was a little extreme. The Christ was loaded down with chains, and the centurions were really laying on the stripes. It certainly would not have been my choice, but I don't believe in interfering too much with children, so I said nothing.

DYSART But Mr Strang did?

DORA He stood it for a while, but one day we had one of our tiffs about religion, and he went straight upstairs, tore it off the boy's wall and threw it in the dustbin. Alan went quite hysterical. He cried for days without stopping – and he was not a crier, you know.

DYSART But he recovered when he was given the photograph of the horse in its place?

DORA He certainly seemed to. At least, he hung it in exactly the same position, and we had no more of that awful weeping.

DYSART Thank you, Mrs Strang. That *is* interesting... Exactly how long ago was that? Can you remember?

DORA It must be five years ago, Doctor. Alan would have been about twelve. How is he, by the way?

DYSART Bearing up.

She rises.

DORA Please give him my love.

DYSART You can see him any time you want, you know.

DORA Perhaps if I could come one afternoon without Mr Strang. He and Alan don't exactly get on at the moment, as you can imagine.

DYSART Whatever you decide, Mrs Strang... Oh, one thing.

DORA Yes?

DYSART Could you describe that photograph of the horse in a little more detail for me? I presume it's still in his bedroom?

DORA Oh, yes. It's a most remarkable picture, really. You very rarely see a horse taken from that angle – absolutely head on. That's what makes it so interesting.

DYSART Why? What does it look like?

DORA Well, it's most extraordinary. It comes out all eyes.

29

DYSART Staring straight at you?

DORA Yes, that's right...

An uncomfortable pause.

I'll come and see him one day very soon, Doctor. Goodbye.

She leaves, and resumes her place by her husband.

DYSART (*to audience*) It was then – that moment – I felt real alarm. What was it? The shadow of a giant head across my desk?... At any rate, the feeling got worse with the stable-owner's visit.

12

Dalton comes in to the square: heavy-set: mid-fifties.

DALTON Dr Dysart?

DYSART Mr Dalton. It's very good of you to come.

DALTON It is, actually. In my opinion the boy should be in prison. Not in a hospital at the tax-payers' expense.

DYSART Please sit down.

Dalton sits.

This must have been a terrible experience for you.

DALTON Terrible? I don't think I'll ever get over it. Jill's had a nervous breakdown.

DYSART Jill?

DALTON The girl who worked for me. Of course, she feels responsible in a way. Being the one who introduced him in the first place.

DYSART He was introduced to the stable by a girl?

DALTON Jill Mason. He met her somewhere, and asked for a job. She told him to come and see me. I wish to Christ she never had.

DYSART But when he first appeared he didn't seem in any way peculiar?

DALTON No, he was bloody good. He'd spend hours with the horses cleaning and grooming them, way over the call of duty. I thought he was a real find.

DYSART Apparently, during the whole time he worked for you, he never actually rode.

DALTON That's true.

DYSART Wasn't that peculiar?

DALTON Very... *If* he didn't.

DYSART What do you mean?

Dalton rises.

DALTON Because on and off, that whole year, I had the feeling the horses were being taken out at night.

DYSART At night?

DALTON There were just odd things I noticed. I mean too often one or other of them would be sweaty first thing in the morning, when it wasn't sick. Very sweaty, too. And its stall wouldn't be near as mucky as it should be if it had been in all night. I never paid it much mind at the time. It was only when I realised I'd been hiring a loony, I came to wonder if he hadn't been riding all the time, behind our backs.

DYSART But wouldn't you have noticed if things had been disturbed?

DALTON Nothing ever was. Still, he's a neat worker. That wouldn't prove anything.

DYSART Aren't the stables locked at night?

DALTON Yes.

DYSART And someone sleeps on the premises?

DALTON Me and my son.

DYSART Two people?

DALTON I'm sorry, Doctor. It's obviously just my fancy. I tell you, this thing has shaken me so bad, I'm liable to believe anything. If there's nothing else, I'll be going.

DYSART Look: even if you were right, why should anyone do that? Why would any boy prefer to ride by himself at night, when he could go off with others during the day.

DALTON Are you asking me? He's a loony, isn't he?

Dalton leaves the square and sits again in his place. Dysart watches him go.

31

ALAN It was *sexy*.

DYSART His tape arrived that evening.

13

Alan is sitting on his bed holding the tape-recorder. Nurse approaches briskly, takes the machine from him – gives it to Dysart in the square – and leaves again, resuming her seat. Dysart switches on the tape.

ALAN That's what you want to know, isn't it? All right: it was. I'm talking about the beach. That time when I was a kid. What I told you about....

Pause. He is in great emotional difficulty.

Dysart sits on the left bench listening, file in hand. Alan rises and stands directly behind him, but on the circle, as if recording the ensuing speech. He never, of course, looks directly at the Doctor.

I was pushed forward on the horse. There was sweat on my legs from his neck. The fellow held me tight, and let me turn the horse which way I wanted. All that power going any way you wanted ... His sides were all warm, and the smell ... Then suddenly I was on the ground, where Dad pulled me. I could have bashed him ...

Pause.

Something else. When the horse first appeared, I looked up into his mouth. It was huge. There was this chain in it. The fellow pulled it, and cream dripped out. I said 'Does it hurt?' And he said – the horse said – said –

He stops, in anguish. Dysart makes a note in his file.

(*desperately*) It was always the same, after that. Every time I heard one clop by, I had to run and see. Up a country lane or anywhere. They sort of pulled me. I couldn't take my eyes off them. Just to watch their skins. The way their necks twist, and sweat shines in the folds ... (*pause*) I can't remember when it started. Mum reading to me about Prince who no one could ride, except one boy. Or the white horse in

Revelations. 'He that sat upon him was called Faithful and True. His eyes were as flames of fire, and he had a name written that no man knew but himself'...Words like reins. Stirrup. Flanks...'Dashing his spurs against his charger's flanks!'... Even the words made me feel –... Years, I never told anyone. Mum wouldn't understand. She likes 'Equitation'. Bowler hats and jodhpurs! 'My grandfather dressed for the horse,' she says. What does that mean? The horse isn't dressed. It's the most naked thing you ever saw! More than a dog or a cat or anything. Even the most broken down old nag has got its *life!* To put a bowler on it is *filthy!*... Putting them through their paces! Bloody gymkhanas!... No one understands!...Except cowboys. They do. I wish I was a cowboy. They're free. They just swing up and then it's miles of grass...I bet all cowboys are *orphans!*...I bet they are!

NURSE Mr Strang to see you, Doctor.

DYSART (*in surprise*) Mr Strang? Show him up, please.

ALAN No one ever says to cowboys 'Receive my meaning'! They wouldn't dare. Or 'God' all the time. (*mimicking his mother*) 'God sees you, Alan. God's got eyes everywhere—'

He stops abruptly.

I'm not doing any more!...I hate this!...You can whistle for anymore. I've had it!

He returns angrily to his bed, throwing the blanket over him. Dysart switches off the tape.

14

Frank Strang comes into the square, his hat in his hand. He is nervous and embarrassed.

DYSART (*welcoming*) Hallo, Mr Strang.

FRANK I was just passing. I hope it's not too late.

DYSART Of course not. I'm delighted to see you.

FRANK My wife doesn't know I'm here. I'd be grateful to you if you didn't enlighten her, if you receive my meaning.

DYSART Everything that happens in this room is confidential, Mr Strang.

FRANK I hope so . . . I hope so . . .

DYSART (*gently*) Do you have something to tell me?

FRANK As a matter of fact I have. Yes.

DYSART Your wife told me about the photograph.

FRANK I know, it's not that! It's *about* that, but it's – worse. . . . I wanted to tell you the other night, but I couldn't in front of Dora. Maybe I should have. It might show her where all that stuff leads to, she drills into the boy behind my back.

DYSART What kind of thing is it?

FRANK Something I witnessed.

DYSART Where?

FRANK At home. About eighteen months ago.

DYSART Go on.

FRANK It was late. I'd gone upstairs to fetch something. The boy had been in bed hours, or so I thought.

DYSART Go on.

FRANK As I came along the passage I saw the door of his bed-room was ajar. I'm sure he didn't know it was. From inside I heard the sound of this chanting.

DYSART Chanting?

FRANK Like the Bible. One of those lists his mother's always reading to him.

DYSART What kind of list?

FRANK Those Begats. So-and-so begat, you know. Genealogy.

DYSART Can you remember what Alan's list sounded like?

FRANK Well, the *sort* of thing. I stood there absolutely astonished. The first word I heard was . . .

ALAN (*rising and chanting*) *Prince!*

DYSART Prince?

FRANK Prince begat Prance. That sort of nonsense.

Alan moves slowly to the centre of the circle, downstage.

ALAN And Prance begat Prankus! And Prankus begat Flankus!

FRANK I looked through the door, and he was standing in the moonlight in his pyjamas, right in front of that big photograph.

DYSART The horse with the huge eyes?

FRANK Right.

ALAN Flankus begat Spankus. And Spankus begat Spunkus the Great, who lived three score years!

FRANK It was all like that. I can't remember the exact names, of course. Then suddenly he knelt down.

DYSART In front of the photograph?

FRANK Yes. Right there at the foot of his bed.

ALAN (*kneeling*) And Legwus begat Neckwus. And Neckwus begat Fleckwus, the King of Spit. And Fleckwus spoke out of his chinkle-chankle!

He bows himself to the ground.

DYSART What?

FRANK I'm sure that was the word. I've never forgotten it. Chinkle-chankle.

Alan raises his head and extends his hands up in glory.

ALAN And he said 'Behold – I give you Equus, my only begotten son!'

DYSART Equus?

FRANK Yes. No doubt of that. He repeated that word several times. 'Equus my only begotten son.'

ALAN (*reverently*) Ek .... wus!

DYSART (*suddenly understanding: almost 'aside'*) Ek. ... Ek. ...

FRANK (*embarrassed*) And then...

DYSART Yes: what?

FRANK He took a piece of string out of his pocket. Made up into a noose. And put it in his mouth.

Alan bridles himself with invisible string, and pulls it back.

And then with his other hand he picked up a coat hanger. A wooden coat hanger, and – and—

DYSART Began to beat himself?

Alan, in mime, begins to thrash himself, increasing the strokes in

35

speed and viciousness.
   Pause.

FRANK You see why I couldn't tell his mother. . . . Religion. Religion's at the bottom of all this!

DYSART What did you do?

FRANK Nothing. I coughed – and went back downstairs.

The boy starts guiltily – tears the string from his mouth – and scrambles back to bed.

DYSART Did you ever speak to him about it later? Even obliquely?

FRANK (*unhappily*) I can't speak of things like that, Doctor. It's not in my nature.

DYSART (*kindly*) No. I see that.

FRANK But I thought you ought to know. So I came.

DYSART (*warmly*) Yes. I'm very grateful to you. Thank you.

Pause.

FRANK Well, that's it . . .

DYSART Is there anything else?

FRANK (*even more embarrassed*) There is actually. One thing.

DYSART What's that?

FRANK On the night that he did it – that awful thing in the stable –

DYSART Yes?

FRANK That very night, he was out with a girl.

DYSART How d'you know that?

FRANK I just know.

DYSART (*puzzled*) Did he tell you?

FRANK I can't say any more.

DYSART I don't quite understand.

FRANK Everything said in here is confidential, you said.

DYSART Absolutely.

FRANK Then ask him. Ask him about taking a girl out, that very night he did it. . . . (*abruptly*) Goodbye, Doctor.

He goes. Dysart looks after him. Frank resumes his seat.

15

Alan gets up and enters the square.

DYSART Alan! Come in. Sit down. (*pleasantly*) What did you do last night?

ALAN Watched telly.

DYSART Any good?

ALAN All right.

DYSART Thanks for the tape. It was excellent.

ALAN I'm not making any more.

DYSART One thing I didn't quite understand. You began to say something about the horse on the beach talking to you.

ALAN That's stupid. Horses don't talk.

DYSART So I believe.

ALAN I don't know what you mean.

DYSART Never mind. Tell me something else. Who introduced you to the stable to begin with?

Pause.

ALAN Someone I met.

DYSART Where?

ALAN Bryson's.

DYSART The shop where you worked?

ALAN Yes.

DYSART That's a funny place for you to be. Whose idea was that?

ALAN Dad.

DYSART I'd thought he'd have wanted you to work with him.

ALAN I haven't the aptitude. And printing's a failing trade. If you receive my meaning.

DYSART (*amused*) I see . . . What did your mother think?

ALAN Shops are common.

DYSART And you?

ALAN I loved it.

DYSART Really?

ALAN (*sarcastic*) Why not? You get to spend every minute with electrical things. It's fun.

Nurse, Dalton and the actors playing horses call out to him as Customers, seated where they are. Their voices are aggressive and demanding. There is a constant background mumbling, made up of trade names, out of which can clearly be distinguished the italicized words, which are shouted out.

CUSTOMER *Philco!*

ALAN (*to Dysart*) Of course it might just drive you off your chump.

CUSTOMER I want to buy a hot-plate. I'm told the *Philco* is a good make!

ALAN I think it is, madam.

CUSTOMER *Remington* ladies' shavers?

ALAN I'm not sure, madam.

CUSTOMER *Robex* tableware?

CUSTOMER *Croydex?*

CUSTOMER *Volex?*

CUSTOMER *Pifco* automatic toothbrushes?

ALAN I'll find out, sir.

CUSTOMER *Beautiflor!*

CUSTOMER *Windolene!*

CUSTOMER I want a *Philco* transistor radio!

CUSTOMER This isn't a *Remington!* I wanted a *Remington!*

ALAN Sorry.

CUSTOMER Are you a dealer for *Hoover?*

ALAN Sorry.

CUSTOMER I wanted the heat retaining *Pifco!*

ALAN *Sorry!*

Jill comes into the square: a girl in her early twenties, pretty and middle class. She wears a sweater and jeans. The mumbling stops.

JILL Hallo.

ALAN Hallo.

JILL Have you any blades for a clipping machine?

ALAN Clipping?

JILL To clip horses.

Pause. He stares at her, open-mouthed.

What's the matter?

ALAN You work at Dalton's stables. I've seen you.

During the following, he mimes putting away a pile of boxes on a shelf in the shop.

JILL I've seen you too, haven't I? You're the boy who's always staring into the yard around lunch-time.

ALAN Me?

JILL You're there most days.

ALAN Not me.

JILL (*amused*) Of course it's you. Mr Dalton was only saying the other day: 'Who's that boy keeps staring in at the door?' Are you looking for a job or something?

ALAN (*eagerly*) Is there one?

JILL I don't know.

ALAN I can only do weekends.

JILL That's when most people ride. We can always use extra hands. It'd mainly be mucking out.

ALAN I don't mind.

JILL Can you ride?

ALAN No ... No ... I don't want to.

She looks at him curiously.

Please.

JILL Come up on Saturday. I'll introduce you to Mr Dalton.

She leaves the square.

DYSART When was this? About a year ago?

ALAN I suppose.

DYSART And she did?

ALAN Yes.

Briskly he moves the three benches to form three stalls in the stable.

16

Rich light falls on the square.

An exultant humming from the Chorus.

Tramping is heard. Three actors playing horses rise from their places. Together they unhook three horse masks from the ladders to left and right, put them on with rigid timing, and walk with swaying horse-motion into the square. Their metal hooves stamp on the wood. Their masks turn and toss high above their heads – as they will do sporadically throughout all horse scenes – making the steel gleam in the light.

For a moment they seem to converge on the boy as he stands in the middle of the stable, but then they swiftly turn and take up positions as if tethered by the head, with their invisible rumps towards him, one by each bench.

Alan is sunk in this glowing world of horses. Lost in wonder, he starts almost involuntarily to kneel on the floor in reverence – but is sharply interrupted by the cheery voice of Dalton, coming into the stable, followed by Jill. The boy straightens up guiltily.

DALTON First thing to learn is drill. Learn it and keep to it. I want this place neat, dry and clean at all times. After you've mucked out, Jill will show you some grooming. What we call strapping a horse.

JILL I think Trooper's got a stone.

DALTON Yes? Let's see.

He crosses to the horse by the left bench, who is balancing one hoof on its tip. He picks up the hoof.

You're right. (*to Alan*) See this? This V here. It's what's called a frog. Sort of shock-absorber. Once you pierce that, it takes ages to heal – so you want to watch for it. You clean it out with this. What we call a hoof-pick.

He takes from his pocket an invisible pick.

Mind how you go with it. It's very sharp. Use it like this.

He quickly takes the stone out.

See?

Alan nods, fascinated.

You'll soon get the hang of it. Jill will look after you. What she doesn't know about stables, isn't worth knowing.

JILL (*pleased*) Oh yes, I'm sure!

DALTON (*handing Alan the pick*) Careful how you go with that.

The main rule is, anything you don't know: ask. Never pretend you know something when you don't. (*smiling*) Actually, the main rule is: enjoy yourself. All right?

ALAN Yes, sir.

DALTON Good lad. See you later.

He nods to them cheerfully, and leaves the square. Alan clearly puts the invisible hoof-pick on the rail, downstage left.

JILL All right, let's start on some grooming. Why don't we begin with him? He looks as if he needs it.

They approach Nugget, who is standing to the right. She pats him. Alan sits and watches her.

This is Nugget. He's my favourite. He's as gentle as a baby, aren't you? But terribly fast if you want him to be.

During the following, she mimes both the actions and the objects, which she picks up from the right bench.

Now this is the dandy, and we start with that. Then you move on to the body brush. This is the most important, and you use it with this curry-comb. Now you always groom the same way: from the ears downward. Don't be afraid to do it hard. The harder you do it, the more the horse loves it. Push it right through the coat: like this.

The boy watches in fascination as she brushes the invisible body of Nugget, scraping the dirt and hair off on to the invisible curry-comb. Now and then the horse mask moves very slightly in pleasure.

Down towards the tail and right through the coat. See how he loves it? I'm giving you a lovely massage, boy, aren't I? ... You try.

She hands him the brush. Gingerly he rises and approaches Nugget. Embarrassed and excited, he copies her movements, inexpertly.

Keep it nice and easy. Never rush. Down towards the tail and right through the coat. That's it. Again. Down towards the tail and right through the coat.... Very good. Now you keep that up for fifteen minutes and then do old Trooper. Will you?

Alan nods.

You've got a feel for it. I can tell. It's going to be nice

41

teaching you. See you later.

She leaves the square and resumes her place. Alan is left alone with the horses.

They all stamp. He approaches Nugget again, and touches the horse's shoulder. The mask turns sharply in his direction. The boy pauses, then moves his hand gently over the outline of the neck and back. The mask is re-assured. It stares ahead unmoving. Then Alan lifts his palm to his face and smells it deeply, closing his eyes.

Dysart rises from his bench, and begins to walk slowly upstage round the circle.

DYSART Was that good? Touching them.

Alan gives a faint groan.

ALAN Mmm.

DYSART It must have been marvellous, being near them at last ...Stroking them...Making them fresh and glossy...Tell me...

Silence. Alan begins to brush Nugget.

How about the girl? Did you like her?

ALAN (*tight*) All right.

DYSART Just all right?

Alan changes his position, moving round Nugget's rump so that his back is to the audience. He brushes harder. Dysart comes downstage around the circle, and finally back to his bench.

Was she friendly?

ALAN Yes.

DYSART Or stand-offish?

ALAN Yes.

DYSART Well which?

ALAN What?

DYSART Which was she?

Alan brushes harder.

Did you take her out? Come on now: tell me. Did you have a date with her?

ALAN What?

DYSART (*sitting*) Tell me if you did.

The boy suddenly explodes in one of his rages.

42

ALAN (*yelling*) TELL ME!
All the masks toss at the noise.
DYSART What?
ALAN *Tell me, tell me, tell me, tell me!*
Alan storms out of the square, and downstage to where Dysart sits. He is raging. During the ensuing, the horses leave by all three openings.

   On and on, sitting there! Nosey Parker! That's all you are!
   Bloody Nosey Parker! Just like Dad. On and on and bloody
   on! Tell me, tell me, tell me!... Answer this. Answer that.
   Never stop! –
He marches round the circle and back into the square. Dysart rises and enters it from the other side.

17

Lights brighten.

DYSART I'm sorry.
Alan slams about what is now the office again, replacing the benches to their usual position.
ALAN All right, it's my turn now. You tell me! Answer me!
DYSART We're not playing that game now.
ALAN We're playing what I say.
DYSART All right. What do you want to know?
He sits.
ALAN Do *you* have dates?
DYSART I told you. I'm married.
Alan approaches him, very hostile.
ALAN I know. Her name's Margaret. She's a dentist! You see,
   I found out! What made you go with her? Did you use to
   bite her hands when she did you in the chair?
The boy sits next to him, close.
DYSART That's not very funny.
ALAN Do you have girls behind her back?
DYSART No.

43

ALAN Then what? Do you fuck her?

DYSART That's enough now.

He rises and moves away.

ALAN Come on, tell me! Tell me, tell me!

DYSART I said that's enough now.

Alan rises too and walks around him.

ALAN I bet you don't. I bet you never touch her. Come on, tell
   me. You've got no kids, have you? Is that because you don't
   fuck?

DYSART (*sharp*) Go to your room. Go on: quick march.

*Pause. Alan moves away from him, insolently takes up a packet of
Dysart's cigarettes from the bench, and extracts one.*

   Give me those cigarettes.

The boy puts one in his mouth.

   (*exploding*) Alan, *give them to me!*

*Reluctantly Alan shoves the cigarette back in the packet, turns and hands
it to him.*

   Now go!

*Alan bolts out of the square, and back to his bed. Dysart, unnerved,
addresses the audience.*

   Brilliant! Absolutely brilliant! The boy's on the run, so he
   gets defensive. What am *I*, then? . . . Wicked little bastard –
   he knew exactly what questions to try. He'd actually march-
   ed himself round the hospital, making enquiries about my
   wife. Wicked and – of course, perceptive. Ever since I made
   that crack about carving up children, he's been aware of me
   in an absolutely specific way. Of course, there's nothing
   novel in that. Advanced neurotics can be dazzling at that
   game. They aim unswervingly at your area of maximum vul-
   nerability . . . Which I suppose is as good a way as any of
   describing Margaret.

He sits. Hesther enters the square.

Light grows warmer.

18

HESTHER Now stop it.

DYSART Do I embarrass you?

HESTHER I suspect you're about to.

Pause.

DYSART My wife doesn't understand me, Your Honour.

HESTHER Do you understand her?

DYSART No. Obviously I never did.

HESTHER I'm sorry. I've never liked to ask but I've always imagined you weren't exactly compatible.

She moves to sit opposite.

DYSART We were. It actually worked for a bit. I mean for both of us. We worked for each other. She actually for me through a kind of briskness. A clear, red-headed, inaccessible briskness which kept me keyed up for months. Mind you, if you're kinky for Northern Hygienic, as I am, you can't find anything much more compelling than a Scottish Lady Dentist.

HESTHER It's *you* who are wicked, you know!

DYSART Not at all: She got exactly the same from me. Antiseptic proficiency. I was like that in those days. We suited each other admirably. I see us in our wedding photo: Doctor and Doctor Mac Brisk. We were brisk in our wooing, brisk in our wedding, brisk in our disappointment. We turned from each other briskly into our separate surgeries: and now there's damn all.

HESTHER You have no children, have you?

DYSART No, we didn't go in for them. Instead, she sits beside our salmon-pink, glazed brick fireplace, and knits things for orphans in a home she helps with. And I sit opposite, turning the pages of art books on Ancient Greece. Occasionally, I still trail a faint scent of my enthusiasm across her path. I pass her a picture of the sacred acrobats of Crete leaping through the horns of running bulls – and she'll say: 'Och, Martin, what an *absurred* thing to be doing! The Highland

45

Games, now there's *norrmal* sport!' Or she'll observe, just after I've told her a story from the Iliad: 'You know, when you come to think of it, Agamemnon and that lot were nothing but a bunch of ruffians from the Gorbals, only with fancy names!' (*He rises*) You get the picture. She's turned into a Shrink. The familiar domestic monster. Margaret Dysart: the Shrink's Shrink.

HESTHER That's cruel, Martin.

DYSART Yes. Do you know what it's like for two people to live in the same house as if they were in different parts of the world? Mentally, she's always in some drizzly kirk of her own inheriting: and I'm in some Doric temple – clouds tearing through pillars – eagles bearing prophecies out of the sky. She finds all that repulsive. All my wife has ever taken from the Mediterranean – from that whole vast intuitive culture – are four bottles of Chianti to make into lamps, and two china condiment donkeys labelled Sally and Peppy.

Pause.

(*more intimately*) I wish there was one person in my life I could show. One instinctive, absolutely unbrisk person I could take to Greece, and stand in front of certain shrines and sacred streams and say 'Look! Life is only comprehensible through a thousand local Gods. And not just the old dead ones with names like Zeus – no, but living Geniuses of Place and Person! And not just Greece but modern England! Spirits of certain trees, certain curves of brick wall, certain chip shops, if you like, and slate roofs – just as of certain frowns in people and slouches... I'd say to them – 'Worship as many as you can see – and more will appear!'... If I had a son, I bet you he'd come out exactly like his mother. Utterly worshipless. Would you like a drink?

HESTHER No, thanks. Actually, I've got to be going. As usual...

DYSART Really?

HESTHER Really. I've got an Everest of papers to get through before bed.

DYSART You never stop, do you?

HESTHER Do you?

DYSART This boy, with his stare. He's trying to save himself through me.

HESTHER I'd say so.

DYSART What am I trying to do to him?

HESTHER Restore him, surely?

DYSART To what?

HESTHER A normal life.

DYSART Normal?

HESTHER It still means something.

DYSART Does it?

HESTHER Of course.

DYSART You mean a normal boy has one head: a normal head has two ears?

HEATHER You know I don't.

DYSART Then what else?

HESTHER (*lightly*) Oh, stop it.

DYSART No, what? You tell me.

HESTHER (*rising: smiling*) I won't be put on the stand like this, Martin. You're really disgraceful! ... (*Pause*) You know what I mean by a normal smile in a child's eyes, and one that isn't – even if I can't exactly define it. Don't you?

DYSART Yes.

HESTHER Then we have a duty to that, surely? Both of us.

DYSART Touché. . . . I'll talk to you.

HESTHER Dismissed?

DYSART You said you had to go.

HESTHER I do ... (*she kisses his cheek*). Thank you for what you're doing. . . . You're going through a rotten patch at the moment. I'm sorry ... I suppose one of the few things one can do is simply hold on to priorities.

DYSART Like what?

HESTHER Oh – children before grown-ups. Things like that.

He contemplates her.

DYSART You're really quite splendid.

47

HESTHER Famous for it. Goodnight.
She leaves him.
DYSART (*to himself – or to the audience*) Normal! . . . Normal!

19

Alan rises and enters the square. He is subdued.

DYSART Good afternoon.
ALAN Afternoon.
DYSART I'm sorry about our row yesterday.
ALAN It was stupid.
DYSART It was.
ALAN What I said, I mean.
DYSART How are you sleeping?
Alan shrugs.
   You're not feeling well, are you?
ALAN All right.
DYSART Would you like to play a game? It could make you feel
   better.
ALAN What kind?
DYSART It's called *Blink*. You have to fix your eyes on some-
   thing: say, that little stain over there on the wall – and I tap
   this pen on the desk. The first time I tap it, you close your
   eyes. The next time you open them. And so on. Close, open,
   close, open, till I say Stop.
ALAN How can that make you feel better?
DYSART It relaxes you. You'll feel as though you're talking to
   me in your sleep.
ALAN It's stupid.
DYSART You don't have to do it, if you don't want to.
ALAN I didn't say I didn't want to.
DYSART Well?
ALAN I don't mind.
DYSART Good. Sit down and start watching that stain. Put

your hands by your sides, and open the fingers wide.

He opens the left bench and Alan sits on the end of it.

The thing is to feel comfortable, and relax absolutely... Are you looking at the stain?

ALAN Yes.

DYSART Right. Now try and keep your mind as blank as possible.

ALAN That's not difficult.

DYSART Ssh. Stop talking... On the first tap, close. On the second, open. Are you ready?

Alan nods. Dysart taps his pen on the wooden rail. Alan shuts his eyes. Dysart taps again. Alan opens them. The taps are evenly spaced. After four of them the sound cuts out, and is replaced by a louder, metallic sound, on tape. Dysart talks through this, to the audience – the light changes to cold – while the boy sits in front of him, staring at the wall, opening and shutting his eyes.

The Normal is the good smile in a child's eyes – all right. It is also the dead stare in a million adults. It both sustains and kills – like a God. It is the Ordinary made beautiful: it is also the Average made lethal. The Normal is the indispensable, murderous God of Health, and I am his Priest. My tools are very delicate. My compassion is honest. I have honestly assisted children in this room. I have talked away terrors and relieved many agonies. But also – beyond question – I have cut from them parts of individuality repugnant to this God, in both his aspects. Parts sacred to rarer and more wonderful Gods. And at what length... sacrifices to Zeus took at the most, surely, sixty seconds each. Sacrifices to the Normal can take as long as sixty months.

The natural sound of the pencil resumes.

Light changes back.

(*to Alan*) Now your eyes are feeling heavy. You want to sleep, don't you? You want a long, deep sleep. Have it. Your head is heavy. Very heavy. Your shoulders are heavy. Sleep.

The pencil stops. Alan's eyes remain shut and his head has sunk on his chest.

Can you hear me?

ALAN Mmm.

DYSART You can speak normally. Say Yes, if you can.

ALAN Yes.

DYSART Good boy. Now raise your head, and open your eyes.

He does so.

Now, Alan, you're going to answer questions I'm going to ask you. Do you understand?

ALAN Yes.

DYSART And when you wake up, you are going to remember everything you tell me. All right?

ALAN Yes.

DYSART Good. Now I want you to think back in time. You are on that beach you told me about. The tide has gone out, and you're making sandcastles. Above you, staring down at you, is that great horse's head, and the cream dropping from it. Can you see that?

ALAN Yes.

DYSART You ask him a question. 'Does the chain hurt?'

ALAN Yes.

DYSART Do you ask him aloud?

ALAN No.

DYSART And what does the horse say back?

ALAN 'Yes.'

DYSART Then what do you say?

ALAN 'I'll take it out for you.'

DYSART And he says?

ALAN 'It never comes out. They have me in chains.'

DYSART Like Jesus?

ALAN Yes!

DYSART Only his name isn't Jesus, is it?

ALAN No.

DYSART What is it?

ALAN No one knows but him and me.

DYSART You can tell me, Alan. Name him.

ALAN Equus.

DYSART Thank you. Does he live in all horses or just some?

ALAN All.

DYSART Good boy. Now: you leave the beach. You're in your bedroom at home. You're twelve years old. You're in front of the picture. You're looking at Equus from the foot of your bed. Would you like to kneel down?

ALAN Yes.

DYSART (*encouragingly*) Go on, then.

Alan kneels.

Now tell me. Why is Equus in chains?

ALAN For the sins of the world.

DYSART What does he say to you?

ALAN 'I see you.' 'I will save you.'

DYSART How?

ALAN 'Bear you away. Two shall be one.'

DYSART Horse and rider shall be one beast?

ALAN One person!

DYSART Go on.

ALAN 'And my chinkle-chankle shall be in thy hand.'

DYSART Chinkle-chankle? That's his mouth chain?

ALAN Yes.

DYSART Good. You can get up... Come on.

Alan rises.

Now: think of the stable. What is the stable? His Temple? His Holy of Holies?

ALAN Yes.

DYSART Where you wash him? Where you tend him, and brush him with many brushes?

ALAN Yes.

DYSART And there he spoke to you, didn't he? He looked at you with his gentle eyes, and spake unto you?

ALAN Yes.

DYSART What did he say? 'Ride me?' 'Mount me, and ride me forth at night'?

ALAN Yes.

DYSART And you obeyed?

ALAN Yes.

DYSART How did you learn? By watching others?

ALAN Yes.

DYSART It must have been difficult. You bounced about?

ALAN Yes.

DYSART But he showed you, didn't he? Equus showed you the way.

ALAN No!

DYSART He didn't?

ALAN He showed me nothing! He's a mean bugger! Ride – or fall! That's Straw Law.

DYSART Straw Law?

ALAN He was born in the straw, and this is his law.

DYSART But you managed? You mastered him?

ALAN Had to!

DYSART And then you rode in secret?

ALAN Yes.

DYSART How often?

ALAN Every three weeks. More, people would notice.

DYSART On a particular horse?

ALAN No.

DYSART How did you get into the stable?

ALAN Stole a key. Had it copied at Bryson's.

DYSART Clever boy.

Alan smiles.

Then you'd slip out of the house?

ALAN Midnight! On the stroke!

DYSART How far's the stable?

ALAN Two miles.

Pause.

DYSART Let's do it! Let's go riding! . . . Now!

He stands up, and pushes in his bench.

You are there now, in front of the stable door.

Alan turns upstage.

That key's in your hand. Go and open it.

20

Alan moves upstage, and mimes opening the door.
 Soft light on the circle.
 Humming from the Chorus: the Equus Noise.
 The horse actors enter, raise high their masks, and put them on all together. They stand around the circle – Nugget in the mouth of the tunnel.

DYSART Quietly as possible. Dalton may still be awake. Sssh...
 Quietly... Good. Now go in.

Alan steps secretly out of the square through the central opening on to the circle, now glowing with a warm light. He looks about him. The horses stamp uneasily: their masks turn towards him.

You are on the inside now. All the horses are staring at you. Can you see them?

ALAN (*excited*) Yes!

DYSART Which one are you going to take?

ALAN Nugget.

Alan reaches up and mimes leading Nugget carefully round the circle downstage with a rope, past all the horses on the right.

DYSART What colour is Nugget?

ALAN Chestnut.

The horse picks his way with care. Alan halts him at the corner of the square.

DYSART What do you do, first thing?

ALAN Put on his sandals.

DYSART Sandals?

He kneels, downstage centre.

ALAN Sandals of majesty!... Made of sack.

He picks up the invisible sandals, and kisses them devoutly.

Tie them round his hooves.

He taps Nugget's right leg: the horse raises it and the boy mimes tying the sack round it.

DYSART All four hooves?

ALAN Yes.

53

DYSART Then?

ALAN Chinkle-chankle.

He mimes picking up the bridle and bit.

He doesn't like it so late, but he takes it for my sake. He bends for me. He stretches forth his neck to it.

Nugget bends his head down. Alan first ritually puts the bit into his own mouth, then crosses, and transfers it into Nugget's. He reaches up and buckles on the bridle. Then he leads him by the invisible reins, across the front of the stage and up round the left side of the circle. Nugget follows obediently.

ALAN Buckle and lead out.

DYSART No saddle?

ALAN Never.

DYSART Go on.

ALAN Walk down the path behind. He's quiet. Always is, this bit. Meek and mild legs. At least till the field. Then there's trouble.

The horse jerks back. The mask tosses.

DYSART What kind?

ALAN Won't go in.

DYSART Why not?

ALAN It's his place of Ha Ha.

DYSART What?

ALAN Ha Ha.

DYSART Make him go into it.

ALAN (*whispering fiercely*) Come on!... Come on!...

He drags the horse into the square as Dysart steps out of it.

21

Nugget comes to a halt staring diagonally down what is now the field. The Equus noise dies away. The boy looks about him.

DYSART (*from the circle*) Is it a big field?

ALAN Huge!

DYSART What's it like?

ALAN Full of mist. Nettles on your feet.

He mimes taking off his shoes – and the sting.

  Ah!

DYSART (*going back to his bench*) You take your shoes off?

ALAN Everything.

DYSART All your clothes?

ALAN Yes.

He mimes undressing completely in front of the horse. When he is finished, and obviously quite naked, he throws out his arms and shows himself fully to his God, bowing his head before Nugget.

DYSART Where do you leave them?

ALAN Tree hole near the gate. No one could find them.

He walks upstage and crouches by the bench, stuffing the invisible clothes beneath it. Dysart sits again on the left bench, downstage beyond the circle.

DYSART How does it feel now?

ALAN (*holds himself*) Burns.

DYSART Burns?

ALAN The mist!

DYSART Go on. Now what?

ALAN The Manbit.

He reaches again under the bench and draws out an invisible stick.

DYSART Manbit?

ALAN The stick for my mouth.

DYSART Your mouth?

ALAN To bite on.

DYSART Why? What for?

ALAN So's it won't happen too quick.

DYSART Is it always the same stick?

ALAN Course. Sacred stick. Keep it in the hole. The Ark of the
  Manbit.

DYSART And now what? . . . What do you do now?

Pause. He rises and approaches Nugget.

ALAN Touch him!

DYSART Where?

55

ALAN (*in wonder*) All over. Everywhere. Belly. Ribs. His ribs are of ivory. Of great value!... His flank is cool. His nostrils open for me. His eyes shine. They can see in the dark... *Eyes!*—

Suddenly he dashes in distress to the farthest corner of the square.

DYSART Go on!... Then?

Pause.

ALAN Give sugar.

DYSART A lump of sugar?

Alan returns to Nugget.

ALAN His Last Supper.

DYSART Last before what?

ALAN Ha Ha.

He kneels before the horse, palms upward and joined together.

DYSART Do you say anything when you give it to him?

ALAN (*offering it*) Take my sins. Eat them for my sake... He always does. *communion*

Nugget bows the mask into Alan's palm, then takes a step back to eat.

And then he's ready?

DYSART You can get up on him now?

ALAN Yes!

DYSART Do it, then. Mount him.

Alan, lying before Nugget, stretches out on the square. He grasps the top of the thin metal pole embedded in the wood. He whispers his God's name ceremonially.

ALAN Equus!... Equus!... Equus!

He pulls the pole upright. The actor playing Nugget leans forward and grabs it. At the same instant all the other horses lean forward around the circle, each placing a gloved hand on the rail. Alan rises and walks right back to the upstage corner, left.

Take me!

He runs and jumps high on to Nugget's back.

(*crying out*) Ah!

DYSART What is it?

ALAN Hurts!

DYSART Hurts?

ALAN Knives in his skin! Little knives – all inside my legs.

Nugget mimes restiveness.

ALAN Stay, Equus. No one said Go!... That's it. He's good. Equus the Godslave, Faithful and True. Into my hands he commends himself – naked in his chinkle-chankle. (*he punches Nugget*) Stop it!... He wants to go so badly.

DYSART Go, then. Leave me behind. Ride away now, Alan. Now!... Now you are alone with Equus.

Alan stiffens his body.

ALAN (*ritually*) Equus – son of Fleckwus – son of Neckwus – Walk.

A hum from the Chorus.

Very slowly the horses standing on the circle begin to turn the square by gently pushing the wooden rail. Alan and his mount start to revolve. The effect, immediately, is of a statue being slowly turned round on a plinth. During the ride however the speed increases, and the light decreases until it is only a fierce spotlight on horse and rider, with the overspill glinting on the other masks leaning in towards them.

Here we go. The King rides out on Equus, mightiest of horses. Only I can ride him. He lets me turn him this way and that. His neck comes out of my body. It lifts in the dark. Equus, my Godslave!... Now the King commands you. Tonight, we ride against them all.

DYSART Who's all?

ALAN My foes and His.

DYSART Who are your foes?

ALAN The Hosts of Hoover. The Hosts of Philco. The Hosts of Pifco. The House of Remington and all its tribe!

DYSART Who are His foes?

ALAN The Hosts of Jodhpur. The Hosts of Bowler and Gymkhana. All those who show him off for their vanity. Tie rosettes on his head for their vanity! Come on, Equus. Let's get them!... *Trot!*

The speed of the turning square increases.

Stead-y! Stead-y! Stead-y! Stead-y! Cowboys are watching! Take off their stetsons. They know who we are. They're admiring

57

us! Bowing low unto us! Come on now – show them! *Canter!*
. . . CANTER!

He whips Nugget.

And Equus the Mighty rose against All!
His <u>enemies</u> scatter, his enemies fall!
TURN!
<u>Trample</u> them, trample them,
Trample them, trample them,
TURN!
TURN!!
TURN!!!

The Equus noise increases in volume.

(*shouting*) WEE! . . . WAA! . . . WONDERFUL! . . .
I'm stiff! Stiff in the wind!
My mane, stiff in the wind!
My flanks! *My* hooves!
Mane on my legs, on my flanks, like whips!
Raw!
Raw!
I'm raw! Raw!
Feel me on you! *On* you! *On* you! *On* you!
I want to be *in* you!
I want to BE you forever and ever!–
Equus, I love you!
Now! –
Bear me away!
<u>Make us One Person!</u>

He rides Equus frantically.

<u>One Person! One Person! One Person! One Person!</u>

He rises up on the horse's back, and calls like a trumpet.

Ha-HA! . . . Ha-HA! . . . Ha-HA!

The trumpet turns to great cries.

HA-HA! HA-HA! HA-HA! HA-HA! HA! . . . HA! . . . HAAAAA!

He twists like a flame.

Silence.

The turning square comes to a stop in the same position it occupied at the opening of the Act.

   Slowly the boy drops off the horse's back on to the ground. He lowers his head and kisses Nugget's hoof. Finally he flings back his head and cries up to him:

AMEN!   *Climax*

Nugget snorts, once.

Blackout

Act Two

22

Darkness.

Lights come slowly up on Alan kneeling in the night at the hooves of Nugget. Slowly he gets up, climbing lovingly up the body of the horse until he can stand and kiss it.

Dysart sits on the downstage bench where he began Act One.

DYSART With one particular horse, called Nugget, he embraces. He showed me how he stands with it afterwards in the night, one hand on its chest, one on its neck, like a frozen tango dancer, inhaling its cold sweet breath. 'Have you noticed,' he said, 'about horses: how they'll stand one hoof on its end, like those girls in the ballet?'

Alan leads Nugget out of the square. Dysart rises. The horse walks away up the tunnel and disappears. The boy comes downstage and sits on the bench Dysart has vacated. Dysart crosses downstage and moves slowly up round the circle, until he reaches the central entrance to the square.

Now he's gone off to rest, leaving me alone with Equus. I can hear the creature's voice. It's calling me out of the black cave of the Psyche. I shove in my dim little torch, and there he stands – waiting for me. He raises his matted head. He opens his great square teeth, and says – (*mocking*) '*Why?* ... Why Me? ... Why – ultimately – Me? ... Do you really imagine you can account for Me? Totally, infallibly, inevitably account for Me? ... Poor Doctor Dysart!'

He enters the square.

Of course I've stared at such images before. Or been stared at by them, whichever way you look at it. And weirdly often now with me the feeling is that *they* are staring at *us* – that in some quite palpable way they precede us. Meaningless, but unsettling ... In either case, this one is the most alarming yet. It asks questions I've avoided all my professional life.

(*Pause*) A child is born into a world of phenomena all equal in their power to enslave. It sniffs – it sucks – it strokes its eyes over the whole uncomfortable range. Suddenly one strikes. Why? Moments snap together like magnets, forging a chain of shackles. Why? I can trace them. I can even, with time, pull them apart again. But why at the start they were ever magnetized at all – just those particular moments of experience and no others – I don't know. *And nor does anyone else.* Yet *if* I don't know – if I can never know that – then what am I doing here? I don't mean clinically doing or socially doing – I mean *fundamentally!* These questions, these Whys, are fundamental – yet they have no place in a consulting room. So then, do I?.. This is the feeling more and more with me – No Place. Displacement.... 'Account for me,' says staring Equus. 'First account for Me!...' I fancy this is more than menopause.

Nurse rushes in.

NURSE Doctor!... Doctor! There's a terrible scene with the Strang boy. His mother came to visit him, and I gave her the tray to take in. He threw it at her. She's saying the most dreadful things.

Alan springs up, down left. Dora springs up, down right. They face each other across the bottom end of the stage. It is observable that at the start of this Act Frank is not sitting beside his wife on their bench. It is hopefully not observable that he is placed among the audience upstage, in the gloom, by the central tunnel.

DORA Don't you dare! *Don't you dare!*

DYSART Is she still there?

NURSE Yes!

He quickly leaves the square, followed by the Nurse. Dora moves towards her son.

DORA Don't you look at me like that! I'm not a doctor, you know, who'll take anything. Don't you dare give me that stare, young man!

She slaps his face. Dysart joins them.

DYSART Mrs Strang!

61

DORA I know your stares. They don't work on me!

DYSART (*to her*) Leave this room.

DORA What did you say?

DYSART I tell you to leave here at once.

Dora hesitates. Then:

DORA Goodbye, Alan.

She walks past her son, and round into the square. Dysart follows her.
Both are very upset. Alan returns to his bench and Nurse to her place.

23

Lights up on the square.

DYSART I must ask you never to come here again.

DORA Do you think I want to? Do you think I want to?

DYSART Mrs Strang, what on earth has got into you? Can't you see the boy is highly distressed?

DORA (*ironic*) Really?

DYSART Of course! He's at a most delicate stage of treatment. He's totally exposed. Ashamed. Everything you can imagine!

DORA (*exploding*) *And me? What about me?... What do you think I am?...* I'm a parent, of course – so it doesn't count. That's a dirty word in here, isn't it, 'parent'?

DYSART You know that's not true.

DORA Oh, I know. I know, all right! I've heard it all my life. It's *our* fault. Whatever happens, *we* did it. Alan's just a little victim. He's really done nothing at all! (*savagely*) What do you have to do in this world to get any sympathy – blind animals?

DYSART Sit down, Mrs Strang.

DORA (*ignoring him: more and more urgently*) Look, Doctor: you don't have to live with this. Alan is one patient to you: one out of many. He's my son. I lie awake every night thinking about it. Frank lies there beside me. I can hear him. Neither of us sleeps all night. You come to us and say Who forbids television? who does what behind whose back? – as if we're criminals. Let me tell you something. We're not criminals. We've done nothing wrong. We loved Alan. We gave him the best love we could. All right, we quarrel sometimes – all parents quarrel – we always make it up. My husband is a good man. He's an upright man, religion or no religion. He cares for his home, for the world, and for his boy. Alan had love and care and treats, and as much fun as any boy in the world. I know about loveless homes: I was a teacher. Our home wasn't loveless. I know about privacy too – not invading a child's privacy. All right, Frank may be at fault there – he digs into him too much – but nothing in excess. He's not a bully... (*gravely*) No, doctor. Whatever's happened has happened *because of Alan*. Alan is himself. Every soul is itself. If you added up everything we ever did to him, from his first day on earth to this, you wouldn't find why he did this terrible thing – because that's *him*: not just all of our things added up. Do you understand what I'm saying? I want you to understand, because I lie awake and awake thinking it out, and I want you to know that I deny it absolutely what he's doing now, staring at me, attacking me for what *he's* done, for what *he* is! (*pause: calmer*) You've got your words, and I've got mine. You call it a complex, I suppose. But if you knew God, Doctor, you would know about the Devil. You'd know the Devil isn't made by what mummy says and daddy says. The Devil's there. It's an old-fashioned word, but a true thing... I'll go. What I did in there was inexcusable. I only know he was my little Alan, and then the Devil came.

She leaves the square, and resumes her place. Dysart watches her go, then leaves himself by the opposite entrance, and approaches Alan.

24

Seated on his bench, the boy glares at him.

DYSART I thought you liked your mother.
Silence.

    She doesn't know anything, you know. I haven't told her what you told me. You do know that, don't you?
ALAN It was lies anyway.
DYSART What?
ALAN You and your pencil. Just a con trick, that's all.
DYSART What do you mean?
ALAN Made me say a lot of lies.
DYSART Did it? . . . Like what?
ALAN All of it. Everything I said. Lot of lies.
Pause.
DYSART I see.
ALAN You ought to be locked up. Your bloody tricks.
DYSART I thought you liked tricks.
ALAN It'll be the drug next. I know.
Dysart turns, sharply.
DYSART What drug?
ALAN I've heard. I'm not ignorant. I know what you get up to in here. Shove needles in people, pump them full of truth drug, so they can't help saying things. That's next, isn't it?
Pause.
DYSART Alan, do you know why you're here?
ALAN So you can give me truth drugs.
He glares at him. Dysart leaves abruptly, and returns to the square.

25

Hesther comes in simultaneously from the other side.

DYSART (*agitated*) He actually thinks they exist! And of course he wants one.

HESTHER It doesn't sound like that to me.

DYSART Of course he does. Why mention them otherwise? He wants a way to speak. To finally tell me what happened in that stable. Tape's too isolated, and hypnosis is a trick. At least that's the pretence.

HESTHER Does he still say that today?

DYSART I haven't seen him. I cancelled his appointment this morning, and let him stew in his own anxiety. Now I am almost tempted to play a real trick on him.

HESTHER (*sitting*) Like what?

DYSART The old placebo.

HESTHER You mean a harmless pill?

DYSART Full of *alleged* Truth Drug. Probably an aspirin.

HESTHER But he'd deny it afterwards. Same thing all over.

DYSART No. Because he's ready to abreact. *release of ideas by bringing them into conscuness*

HESTHER Abreact?

DYSART Live it all again. He won't be able to deny it after that, because he'll have shown me. Not just told me – but acted it out in front of me.

HESTHER Can you get him to do that?

DYSART I think so. He's nearly done it already. Under all that glowering, he trusts me. Do you realise that?

HESTHER (*warmly*) I'm sure he does.

DYSART Poor bloody fool.

HESTHER Don't start that again.

Pause.

DYSART (*quietly*) Can you think of anything worse one can do to anybody than take away their worship?

HESTHER Worship?

DYSART Yes, that word again!

HESTHER Aren't you being a little extreme?

DYSART Extremity's the point.

HESTHER Worship isn't destructive, Martin. I know that.

DYSART I don't. I only know it's the core of his life. What else has he got? Think about him. He can hardly read. He knows no physics or engineering to make the world real for him. No paintings to show him how others have enjoyed it. No music except television jingles. No history except tales from a desperate mother. No friends. Not one kid to give him a joke, or make him know himself more moderately. He's a modern citizen for whom society doesn't exist. He lives *one hour* every three weeks – howling in a mist. And after the service kneels to a slave who stands over him obviously and unthrowably his master. With my body I thee worship!... Many men have less vital relationships with their wives.

Pause.

HESTHER All the same, they don't usually blind their wives, do they?

DYSART Oh, come on!

HESTHER Well, do they?

DYSART (*sarcastically*) You mean he's dangerous? A violent, dangerous madman who's going to run round the country doing it again and again?

HESTHER I mean he's in pain, Martin. He's been in pain for most of his life. That much, at least, you *know*.

DYSART Possibly.

HESTHER *Possibly?!*... That cut-off little figure you just described must have been in pain for years.

DYSART (*doggedly*) Possibly.

HESTHER And you can take it away.

DYSART Still – possibly.

HESTHER Then that's enough. That simply has to be enough for you, surely?

DYSART No!

HESTHER Why not?

DYSART Because it's his.

HESTHER I don't understand.

DYSART His pain. His own. He made it.

Pause.

(*earnestly*) Look ... to go through life and call it yours – *your life* – you first have to get your own pain. Pain that's unique to you. You can't just dip into the common bin and say 'That's enough!' . . . He's done that. All right, he's sick. He's full of misery and fear. He was dangerous, and could be again, though I doubt it. But that boy has known a passion more ferocious than I have felt in any second of my life. And, let me tell you something: I envy it.

HESTHER You can't.

DYSART (*vehemently*) Don't you see? That's the Accusation! That's what his stare has been saying to me all this time. '*At least I galloped! When did you?*' . . . (*simply*) I'm jealous, Hesther. Jealous of Alan Strang.

HESTHER That's absurd.

DYSART Is it? . . . I go on about my wife. That smug woman by the fire. Have you thought of the fellow on the other side of it? The finicky, critical husband looking through his art books on mythical Greece. What worship has *he* ever known? Real worship! Without worship you shrink, it's as brutal as that . . . I shrank my *own* life. No one can do it for you. I settled for being pallid and provincial, out of my own eternal timidity. The old story of bluster, and do bugger-all . . . I imply that we can't have children: but actually, it's only me. I had myself tested behind her back. The lowest sperm count you could find. And I never told her. That's all I need – her sympathy mixed with resentment . . . I tell everyone Margaret's the puritan, I'm the pagan. Some pagan! Such wild returns I make to the womb of civilization. Three weeks a year in the Peleponnese, every bed booked in advance, every meal paid for by vouchers, cautious jaunts in hired Fiats, suitcase crammed with Kao-Pectate! Such a fantastic surrender to the primitive. And I use that word endlessly: 'primitive'. 'Oh, the primitive world,' I say. 'What instinctual truths were lost with it!' And while I sit there, baiting a poor unimaginative woman with the word, that freaky boy tries to conjure the reality! I sit looking at pages of centaurs trampling the soil of Argos – and outside my window he is trying to *become one*, in a Hampshire field! . . . I watch that woman knitting, night after night – a woman I haven't *kissed* in six years – and he stands in the dark for an hour, sucking the sweat off his God's hairy cheek! (*pause*) Then in the morning, I put away my books on the cultural shelf, close up the Kodachrome snaps of Mount Olympus, touch my reproduction statue of Dionysus for luck – and go off to hospital to treat him for insanity. Do you see?

HESTHER The boy's in pain, Martin. That's all I see. In the end . . . I'm sorry.

He looks at her. Alan gets up from his bench and stealthily places an envelope in the left-hand entrance of the square, then goes back and sits with his back to the audience, as if watching television.

Hesther rises.

HESTHER That stare of his. Have you thought it might not be accusing you at all?

DYSART What then?

HESTHER Claiming you.

DYSART For what?

HESTHER (*mischievously*) A new God.

Pause.

DYSART Too conventional, for him. Finding a religion in Psychiatry is really for very ordinary patients.

She laughs.

HESTHER Maybe he just wants a new Dad. Or is that too conventional too? . . . Since you're questioning your profession anyway, perhaps you ought to try it and see.

DYSART (*amused*) I'll talk to you.

HESTHER Goodbye.

She smiles, and leaves him.

26

Dysart becomes aware of the letter lying on the floor. He picks it up, opens and reads it.

ALAN (*speaking stiffly, as Dysart reads*) 'It is all true, what I said after you tapped the pencil. I'm sorry if I said different. Post Scriptum: I know why I'm in here.'

Pause.

DYSART (*calling, joyfully*) Nurse!

Nurse comes in.

NURSE Yes, Doctor?

DYSART (*trying to conceal his pleasure*) Good evening!

NURSE You're in late tonight.

DYSART Yes!... Tell me, is the Strang boy in bed yet?

NURSE Oh, no, Doctor. He's bound to be upstairs looking at television. He always watches to the last possible moment. He doesn't like going to his room at all.

DYSART You mean he's still having nightmares?

NURSE He had a bad one last night.

DYSART Would you ask him to come down here, please?

NURSE (*faint surprise*) Now?

DYSART I'd like a word with him.

NURSE (*puzzled*) Very good, Doctor.

DYSART If he's not back in his room by lights out, tell Night Nurse not to worry. I'll see he gets back to bed all right. And would you phone my home and tell my wife I may be in late?

NURSE Yes, Doctor.

DYSART Ask him to come straight away, please.

Nurse goes to the bench, taps Alan on the shoulder, whispers her message in his ear, and returns to her place. Alan stands up and pauses for a second – then steps into the square.

27

He stands in the doorway, depressed.

DYSART Hallo.
ALAN Hallo.

DYSART I got your letter. Thank you. (*pause*) Also the Post Scriptum.

ALAN (*defensively*) That's the right word. My mum told me. It's Latin for 'After-writing'.

DYSART How are you feeling?

ALAN All right.

DYSART I'm sorry I didn't see you today.

ALAN You were fed up with me.

DYSART Yes. (*pause*) Can I make it up to you now?

ALAN What d'you mean?

DYSART I thought we'd have a session.

ALAN (*startled*) Now?

DYSART Yes! At dead of night!... Better than going to sleep, isn't it?

The boy flinches.

Alan – look. Everything I say has a trick or a catch. Everything I do is a trick or a catch. That's all I know to do. But they work – and you know that. Trust me.

Pause.

ALAN You got another trick, then?

DYSART Yes.

ALAN A truth drug?

DYSART If you like.

ALAN What's it do?

DYSART Make it easier for you to talk.

ALAN Like you can't help yourself?

DYSART That's right. Like you have to speak the truth at all costs. And all of it.

Pause.

ALAN (*slyly*) Comes in a needle, doesn't it?

DYSART No.

ALAN Where is it?

DYSART (*indicating his pocket*) In here.

ALAN Let's see.

Dysart solemnly takes a bottle of pills out of his pocket.

DYSART There.

ALAN (*suspicious*) That really it?

DYSART It is ... Do you want to try it?

ALAN No.

DYSART I think you do.

ALAN I don't. Not at all.

DYSART Afterwards you'd sleep. You'd have no bad dreams all
night. Probably many nights, from then on ...

Pause.

ALAN How long's it take to work?

DYSART It's instant. Like coffee.

ALAN (*half believing*) It isn't!

DYSART I promise you ... Well?

ALAN Can I have a fag?

DYSART Pill first. Do you want some water?

ALAN No.

*Dysart shakes one out on to his palm. Alan hesitates for a second – then
takes it and swallows it.*

DYSART Then you can chase it down with this. Sit down.

He offers him a cigarette, and lights it for him.

ALAN (*nervous*) What happens now?

DYSART We wait for it to work.

ALAN What'll I feel first?

DYSART Nothing much. After a minute, about a hundred green
snakes should come out of that cupboard singing the Hallelujah Chorus.

ALAN (*annoyed*) I'm serious!

DYSART (*earnestly*) You'll feel nothing. Nothing's going to happen now but what you want to happen. You're not going to
say anything to me but what you want to say. Just relax. Lie
back and finish your fag.

Alan stares at him. Then accepts the situation, and lies back.

DYSART Good boy.

ALAN I bet this room's heard some funny things.

DYSART It certainly has.

ALAN I like it.

DYSART This room?

71

ALAN Don't you?

DYSART Well, there's not much to like, is there?

ALAN How long am I going to be in here?

DYSART It's hard to say. I quite see you want to leave.

ALAN No.

DYSART You don't?

ALAN Where would I go?

DYSART Home....

The boy looks at him. Dysart crosses and sits on the rail upstage, his feet on the bench. A pause.

Actually, I'd like to leave this room and never see it again in my life.

ALAN (*surprise*) Why?

DYSART I've been in it too long.

ALAN Where would you go?

DYSART Somewhere.

ALAN Secret?

DYSART Yes. There's a sea – a great sea – I love... It's where the Gods used to go to bathe.

ALAN What Gods?

DYSART The old ones. Before they died.

ALAN Gods don't die.

DYSART Yes, they do. *signifies the end of the worshipping*

Pause.

There's a village I spent one night in, where I'd like to live. It's all white.

ALAN How would you Nosey Parker, though? You wouldn't have a room for it any more.

DYSART I wouldn't mind. I don't actually enjoy being a Nosey Parker, you know.

ALAN Then why do it?

DYSART Because you're unhappy.

ALAN So are you.

Dysart looks at him sharply. Alan sits up in alarm.

Oooh, I didn't mean that!

DYSART Didn't you?

ALAN Here – is that how it works? Things just slip out, not feeling anything?

DYSART That's right.

ALAN But it's so quick!

DYSART I told you: it's instant.

ALAN (*delighted*) It's wicked, isn't it? I mean, you can say anything under it.

DYSART Yes.

ALAN Ask me a question.

DYSART Tell me about Jill.

Pause. The boy turns away.

ALAN There's nothing to tell.

DYSART Nothing?

ALAN No.

DYSART Well, for example – is she pretty? You've never described her.

ALAN She's all right.

DYSART What colour hair?

ALAN Dunno.

DYSART Is it long or short?

ALAN Dunno.

DYSART (*lightly*) You must know that.

ALAN I don't remember. *I don't!*

Dysart rises and comes down to him. He takes the cigarette out of his hand.

DYSART (*firmly*) Lie back ....Now listen. You have to do this. And now. You are going to tell me everything that happened with this girl. And not just *tell* me – *show* me. Act it out, if you like – even more than you did when I tapped the pencil. I want you to feel free to do absolutely anything in this room. The pill will help you. I will help you ... Now, where does she live?

A long pause.

ALAN (*tight*) Near the stables. About a mile.

Dysart steps down out of the square as Jill enters it. He sits again on the downstage bench.

28

The light grows warmer.

JILL It's called The China Pantry.
She comes down and sits casually on the rail. Her manner is open and lightly provocative. During these scenes Alan acts directly with her, and never looks over at Dysart when he replies to him.
  When Daddy disappeared, she was left without a bean. She had to earn her own living. I must say she did jolly well, considering she was never trained in business.

DYSART What do you mean, 'disappeared'?

ALAN *(to Dysart)* He ran off. No one ever saw him again.

JILL Just left a note on her dressing table saying 'Sorry. I've had it.' Just like that. She never got over it. It turned her right off men. All my dates have to be sort of secret. I mean, she knows about them, but I can't ever bring anyone back home. She's so rude to them.

ALAN *(to Dysart)* She was always looking.

DYSART At you?

ALAN *(to Dysart)* Saying stupid things.
She jumps off the bench.

JILL You've got super eyes.

ALAN *(to Dysart)* Anyway, *she* was the one who had them.
She sits next to him. Embarrassed, the boy tries to move away as far as he can.

JILL There was an article in the paper last week saying what points about boys fascinate girls. They said Number One is bottoms. I think it's eyes every time ... They fascinate you too, don't they?

ALAN Me?

JILL *(sly)* Or is it only horse's eyes?

ALAN *(startled)* What d'you mean?

JILL I saw you staring into Nugget's eyes yesterday for ages. I spied on you through the door!

ALAN *(hotly)* There must have been something in it!

74

JILL You're a real Man of Mystery, aren't you?

ALAN (*to Dysart*) Sometimes, it was like she knew.

DYSART Did you ever hint?

ALAN (*to Dysart*) Course not!

JILL I love horses' eyes. The way you can see yourself in them. D'you find them sexy?

ALAN (*outraged*) What?!

JILL Horses.

ALAN Don't be daft!

He springs up, and away from her.

JILL Girls do. I mean, they go through a period when they pat them and kiss them a lot. I know *I* did. I suppose it's just a substitute, really.

ALAN (*to Dysart*) That kind of thing, all the time. Until one night . . .

DYSART Yes? What?

ALAN (*to Dysart: defensively*) She did it! Not me. It was her idea, the whole thing! . . . She got me into it!

DYSART What are you saying? 'One night': go on from there.

A pause.

ALAN (*to Dysart*) Saturday night. We were just closing up.

JILL How would you like to take me out?

ALAN What?

JILL (*coolly*) How would you like to take me out tonight?

ALAN I've got to go home.

JILL What for?

He tries to escape upstage.

ALAN They expect me.

JILL Ring up and say you're going out.

ALAN I can't.

JILL Why?

ALAN They expect me.

JILL Look. Either we go out together and have some fun, or you go back to your boring home, *as usual*, and I go back to mine. That's the situation, isn't it?

ALAN Well . . . where would we go?

75

JILL The pictures! There's a skinflick over in Winchester! I've never seen one, have you?

ALAN No.

JILL Wouldn't you like to? *I* would. All those heavy Swedes, panting at each other! . . . What d'you say?

ALAN (*grinning*) Yeh! . . .

JILL Good! . . .

He turns away.

DYSART Go on, please.

He steps off the square.

ALAN (*to Dysart*) I'm tired now!

DYSART Come on now. You can't stop there.

He storms round the circle to Dysart, and faces him directly.

ALAN I'm *tired!* I want to go to bed!

DYSART (*sharply*) Well, you can't. I want to hear about the film.

ALAN (*hostile*) Hear what? . . . *What?* . . . It was bloody awful!

The actors playing horses come swiftly on to the square, dressed in sports coats or raincoats. They move the benches to be parallel with the audience, and sit on them – staring out front.

DYSART Why?

ALAN Nosey Parker!

DYART *Why?*

ALAN *Because!* . . . Well – we went into the Cinema!

29

A burst of rock music, instantly fading down. Lights darken.

Alan re-enters the square. Jill rises and together they grope their way to the downstage bench, as if in a dark auditorium.

ALAN (*to Dysart*) The whole place was full of men. Jill was the only girl.

They push by a patron seated at the end, and sit side by side, staring up at the invisible screen, located above the heads of the main audience.

A spotlight hits the boy's face.

We sat down and the film came on. It was daft. Nothing happened for ages. There was this girl Brita, who was six-teen. She went to stay in this house, where there was an older boy. He kept giving her looks, but she ignored him completely. In the end she took a shower. She went into the bathroom and took off all her clothes. The lot. Very slowly. . . . What she didn't know was the boy was looking through the door all the time. . . . (*he starts to become excited*) It was fantastic! The water fell on her breasts, bouncing down her . . . .

Frank steps into the square furtively from the back, hat in hand, and stands looking about for a place.

DYSART Was that the first time you'd seen a girl naked?

ALAN (*to Dysart*) Yes! You couldn't see everything, though . . . . (*looking about him*) All round me they were all looking. All the men – staring up like they were in church. Like they were a sort of congregation. And then – (*he sees his father*) Ah!

At the same instant Frank sees him.

FRANK Alan!

ALAN God!

JILL What is it?

ALAN *Dad!*

JILL *Where?*

ALAN At the back! *He saw me!*

JILL You sure?

ALAN Yes!

FRANK (*calling*) Alan!

ALAN Oh God!

He tries to hide his face in the girl's shoulder. His father comes down the aisle towards him.

FRANK Alan! You can hear me! Don't pretend!

PATRONS Sssh!

FRANK (*approaching the row of seats*) Do I have to come and fetch you out? . . . Do I? . . .

Cries of 'Sssh!' and 'Shut up!'

Do I, Alan?

ALAN (*through gritted teeth*) Oh fuck!

He gets up as the noise increases. Jill gets up too and follows him.

DYSART You went?

ALAN (*to Dysart*) What else could I do? He kept shouting. Everyone was saying Shut up!

They go out, right, through the group of Patrons – who rise protesting as they pass, quickly replace the benches and leave the square.

Dysart enters it.

30

Light brightens from the cinema, but remains cold: streets at night.

The three walk round the circle downstage in a line: Frank leading, wearing his hat. He halts in the middle of the left rail, and stands staring straight ahead of him, rigid with embarrassment. Alan is very agitated.

ALAN (*to Dysart*) We went into the street, all three of us. It was weird. We just stood there by the bus stop – like we were three people in a queue, and we didn't know each other. Dad was all white and sweaty. He didn't look at us at all. It must have gone on for about five minutes. I tried to speak. I said – (*to his father*) I – I – I've never been there before. Honest...Never... (*to Dysart*) He didn't seem to hear. Jill tried.

JILL It's true, Mr Strang. It wasn't Alan's idea to go there. It was mine.

ALAN (*to Dysart*) He just went on staring, straight ahead. It was awful.

JILL I'm not shocked by films like that. I think they're just silly.

ALAN (*to Dysart*) The bus wouldn't come. We just stood and stood.... Then suddenly he spoke.

Frank takes off his hat.

FRANK (*stiffly*) I'd like you to know something. Both of you. I came here tonight to see the Manager. He asked me to call on him for business purposes. I happen to be a printer, Miss. A picture house needs posters. That's entirely why I'm here. To discuss posters. While I was waiting I happened to glance in, that's all. I can only say I'm going to complain to the council. I had no idea they showed films like this. I'm certainly going to refuse my services.

JILL (*kindly*) Yes, of course.

FRANK So long as that's understood.

ALAN (*to Dysart*) Then the bus came along.

FRANK Come along, now Alan.

He moves away downstage.

ALAN No.

FRANK (*turning*) No fuss, please. Say Goodnight to the young lady.

ALAN (*timid but firm*) No. I'm stopping here ... I've got to see her home ... It's proper.

Pause.

FRANK (*as dignified as possible*) Very well. I'll see you when you choose to return. Very well then ... Yes ...

He walks back to his original seat, next to his wife. He stares across the square at his son – who stares back at him. Then, slowly, he sits.

ALAN (*to Dysart*) And he got in, and we didn't. He sat down and looked at me through the glass. And I saw ...

DYSART (*soft*) What?

ALAN (*to Dysart*) His face. It was scared.

DYSART Of you?

ALAN (*to Dysart*) It was terrible. We had to walk home. Four miles. I got the shakes.

DYSART You were scared too?

ALAN (*to Dysart*) It was like a hole had been drilled in my tummy. A hole – right here. And the air was getting in!

He starts to walk upstage, round the circle.

31

The girl stays still.

JILL (*aware of other people looking*) Alan ...

ALAN (*to Dysart*) People kept turning round in the street to look.

JILL Alan!

ALAN (*to Dysart*) I kept seeing him, just as he drove off. Scared of me.... And me scared of *him*.... I kept thinking – all those airs he put on! ... 'Receive my meaning. Improve your mind!' ... All those nights he said he'd be in late. 'Keep my supper hot, Dora!' 'Your poor father: he works so hard!' ... Bugger! Old bugger! ... Filthy old bugger!

He stops, clenching his fists.

JILL Hey! Wait for me!

She runs after him. He waits.

What are you thinking about?

ALAN Nothing.

JILL Mind my own beeswax?

She laughs.

ALAN (*to Dysart*) And suddenly she began to laugh.

JILL I'm sorry. But it's pretty funny, when you think of it.

ALAN (*bewildered*) What?

JILL Catching him like that! I mean, it's terrible – but it's very funny.

ALAN Yeh!

He turns from her.

JILL No, wait! ... I'm sorry. I know you're upset. But it's not the end of the world, is it? I mean, what was he doing? Only what we were. Watching a silly film. It's a case of like father like son, I'd say! ... I mean, when that girl was taking a shower, you were pretty interested, weren't you?

He turns round and looks at her.

We keep saying old people are square. Then when they suddenly aren't – we don't like it!

DYSART What did you think about that?

ALAN (*to Dysart*) I don't know. I kept looking at all the people in the street. They were mostly men coming out of pubs. I suddenly thought – *they all do it! All of them!* . . . They're not just Dads – they're people with pricks! . . . And Dad – he's not just Dad either. He's a man with a prick too. You know, I'd never thought about it.

Pause.

We went into the country.

He walks again. Jill follows. They turn the corner and come downstage, right.

We kept walking. I just thought about Dad, and how he was nothing special – just a poor old sod on his own.

He stops.

(*to Jill: realising it*) Poor old sod!

JILL That's right!

ALAN (*grappling with it*) I mean, what else has he got? . . . He's got mum, of course, but well – she – she – she—

JILL She doesn't give him anything?

ALAN That's right. I bet you . . . She doesn't give him anything. That's right . . . That's really right! . . . She likes Ladies and Gentlemen. Do you understand what I mean?

JILL (*mischievously*) Ladies and gentlemen aren't naked?

ALAN That's right! Never! . . . *Never!* That would be disgusting! She'd have to put bowler hats on them! . . . Jodhpurs!

She laughs.

DYSART Was that the first time you ever thought anything like that about your mother? . . . I mean, that she was unfair to your dad?

ALAN (*to Dysart*) Absolutely!

DYSART How did you feel?

ALAN (*to Dysart*) Sorry. I mean for him. Poor old sod, that's what I felt – he's just like me! He hates ladies and gents just like me! Posh things – and la-di-da. He goes off by himself at night, and does his own secret thing which no one'll know about, just like me! There's no difference – he's just the

81

*× No need to be ashamed of his feelings
o desires*

same as me – just the same!––

He stops in distress, then bolts back a little upstage.

Christ!

DYSART (*sternly*) Go on.

ALAN (*to Dysart*) I can't.

DYSART Of course you can. You're doing wonderfully.

ALAN (*to Dysart*) No, please. *Don't make me!*

DYSART (*firm*) Don't think: just answer. You were happy at that second, weren't you? When you realised about your dad. How lots of people have secrets, not just you?

ALAN (*to Dysart*) Yes.

DYSART You felt sort of free, didn't you? I mean, free to do anything?

ALAN (*to Dysart, looking at Jill*) Yes!

DYSART What was she doing?

ALAN (*to Dysart*) Holding my hand.

DYSART And that was good?

ALAN (*to Dysart*) Oh, yes!

DYSART Remember what you thought. *As if it's happening to you now. This very moment . . .* What's in your head?

ALAN (*to Dysart*) Her eyes. *She's the one with eyes!* . . . I keep looking at them, because I really want––

DYSART To look at her breasts?

ALAN (*to Dysart*) Yes.

DYSART Like in the film.

ALAN (*to Dysart*) Yes . . . Then she starts to scratch my hand.

JILL You're really very nice, you know that?

ALAN (*to Dysart*) Moving her nails on the back. Her face so warm. Her eyes.

DYSART You want her very much?

ALAN (*to Dysart*) Yes . . .

JILL I love your eyes.

She kisses him.

(*whispering*) Let's go!

ALAN Where?

JILL I know a place. It's right near here.

ALAN Where?

JILL Surprise!...Come on!

She darts away round the circle, across the stage and up the left side.
   Come *on!*

ALAN (*to Dysart*) She runs ahead. I follow. And then – and
   then—!

He halts.

DYSART What?

ALAN (*to Dysart*) I see what she means.

DYSART What?...Where are you?...Where has she taken
   you?

ALAN (*to Jill*) The Stables?

JILL Of course!

32

Chorus makes a warning hum.

   *The horses-actors enter, and ceremonially put on their masks – first
raising them high above their heads. Nugget stands in the central tunnel.*

ALAN (*recoiling*) No!

JILL Where else? They're perfect!

ALAN No!

He turns his head from her.

JILL Or do you want to go home now and face your dad?

ALAN No!

JILL Then come on!

*He edges nervously past the horse standing at the left, which turns its
neck and even moves a challenging step after him.*

ALAN Why not your place?

JILL I can't. Mother doesn't like me bringing back boys. I told
   you.... Anyway, the Barn's better.

ALAN No!

JILL All that straw. It's cosy.

ALAN No.

JILL *Why not?*

ALAN Them!

JILL Dalton will be in bed . . . What's the matter? . . . Don't you want to?

ALAN (*aching to*) Yes!

JILL So?

ALAN (*desperate*) *Them! . . . Them! . . .*

JILL *Who?*

ALAN (*low*) Horses.

JILL *Horses? . . .* You're really dotty, aren't you? . . . What do you mean?

He starts shaking.

Oh, you're freezing . . . Let's get under the straw. You'll be warm there.

ALAN (*pulling away*) No!

JILL What on earth's the matter with you? . . .

Silence. He won't look at her.

Look, if the sight of horses offends you, my lord, we can just shut the door. You won't have to see them. All right?

DYSART What door is that? In the barn?

ALAN (*to Dysart*) Yes.

DYSART So what do you do? You go in?

ALAN (*to Dysart*) Yes.

33

A rich light falls.

Furtively Alan enters the square from the top end, and Jill follows. The horses on the circle retire out of sight on either side. Nugget retreats up the tunnel and stands where he can just be glimpsed in the dimness.

DYSART Into the Temple? The Holy of Holies?

ALAN (*to Dysart: desperate*) What else can I do? . . . I can't say! I can't tell her . . . (*to Jill*) Shut it tight.

JILL All right . . . You're crazy.

ALAN Lock it.

JILL Lock?

ALAN Yes.

JILL It's just an old door. What's the matter with you? They're in their boxes. They can't get out ... Are you all right?

ALAN Why?

JILL You look weird.

ALAN *Lock it!*

JILL Ssssh! D'you want to wake up Dalton? ... Stay there, idiot.

She mimes locking a heavy door, upstage.

DYSART Describe the barn, please.

ALAN (*walking round it: to Dysart*) Large room. Straw every-where. Some tools ... (*as if picking it up off the rail where he left it in Act One*) A hoof pick! ...

He 'drops' it hastily, and dashes away from the spot.

DYSART Go on.

ALAN (*to Dysart*) At the end this big door. Behind it—

DYSART Horses.

ALAN (*to Dysart*) Yes.

DYSART How many?

ALAN (*to Dysart*) Six.

DYSART Jill closes the door so you can't see them?

ALAN (*to Dysart*) Yes.

DYSART And then? ... What happens now? ... Come on, Alan. Show me.

JILL See, it's all shut. There's just us ... Let's sit down. Come on.

They sit together on the same bench, left.

Hallo.

ALAN (*quickly*) Hallo.

She kisses him lightly. He responds. Suddenly a faint trampling of hooves, off-stage, makes him jump up.

JILL What is it?

He turns his head upstage, listening.

Relax. There's no one there. Come here.

She touches his hand. He turns to her again.

You're very gentle. I love that...

ALAN So are you...I mean...

He kisses her spontaneously. The hooves trample again, harder. He breaks away from her abruptly towards the upstage corner.

JILL (*rising*) What is it?

ALAN Nothing!

She moves towards him. He turns and moves past her. He is clearly distressed. She contemplates him for a moment.

JILL (*gently*) Take your sweater off.

ALAN What?

JILL I will, if you will.

He stares at her. A pause.

She lifts her sweater over her head: he watches – then unzips his. They each remove their shoes, their socks, and their jeans. Then they look at each other diagonally across the square, in which the light is gently increasing.

ALAN You're...You're very...

JILL So are you.... (*pause*) Come here.

He goes to her. She comes to him. They meet in the middle, and hold each other, and embrace.

ALAN (*to Dysart*) She put her mouth in mine. It was lovely! Oh, it was lovely!

They burst into giggles. He lays her gently on the floor in the centre of the square, and bends over her eagerly.

Suddenly the noise of Equus fills the place. Hooves smash on wood. Alan straightens up, rigid. He stares straight ahead of him over the prone body of the girl.

DYSART Yes, what happened then, Alan?

ALAN (*to Dysart: brutally*) I put it in her!

DYSART Yes?

ALAN (*to Dysart*) I put it in her.

DYSART You did?

ALAN(*to Dysart*) Yes!

DYSART Was it easy?

ALAN (*to Dysart*) Yes.

DYSART Describe it.

ALAN (*to Dysart*) I told you.

DYSART More exactly.

ALAN (*to Dysart*) I put it in her!

DYSART Did you?

ALAN (*to Dysart*) All the way!

DYSART Did you, Alan?

ALAN (*to Dysart*) All the way. I shoved it. I put it in her all the way.

DYSART Did you?

ALAN (*to Dysart*) Yes!

DYSART Did you?

ALAN (*to Dysart*) Yes!...Yes!

DYSART Give me the TRUTH!...Did you?...*Honestly?*

ALAN (*to Dysart*) Fuck off!

He collapses, lying upstage on his face. Jill lies on her back motionless, her head downstage, her arms extended behind her. A pause.

DYSART (*gently*) What was it? You couldn't? Though you wanted to very much?

ALAN (*to Dysart*) I couldn't...see her.

DYSART What do you mean?

ALAN (*to Dysart*) Only Him. Every time I kissed her – *He* was in the way.

DYSART Who?

Alan turns on his back.

ALAN (*to Dysart*) You *know* who!...When I touched her, I felt *Him*. Under me...His side, waiting for my hand...His flanks...I refused him. I looked. I looked right at her... and I couldn't do it. When I shut my eyes, I saw Him at once. The streaks on his belly...(*with more desperation*) I couldn't feel *her* flesh at all! I wanted the foam off his neck. His sweaty hide. Not flesh. *Hide! Horse-hide!*...Then I couldn't even kiss her.

Jill sits up.

JILL What is it?

ALAN (*dodging her hand*) No!

87

He scrambles up and crouches in the corner against the rails, like a little beast in a cage.

JILL Alan!

ALAN Stop it!

Jill gets up.

JILL It's all right... It's all right... Don't worry about it. It often happens – honest... There's nothing wrong. I don't mind, you know... I don't at all.

He dashes past her downstage.

Alan, look at me... Alan?... Alan!

He collapses again by the rail.

ALAN Get out!...

JILL What?

ALAN (*soft*) Out!

JILL There's nothing wrong: believe me! It's very common.

ALAN *Get out!*

He snatches up the invisible pick.

GET OUT!

JILL Put that down!

ALAN Leave me alone!

JILL Put that down, Alan. It's very dangerous. Go on, please – drop it.

He 'drops' it, and turns from her.

ALAN You ever tell anyone. Just you tell...

JILL Who do you think I am?... I'm your friend – Alan...

She goes towards him.

Listen: you don't have to do anything. Try to realize that. Nothing at all. Why don't we just lie here together in the straw. And talk.

ALAN (*low*) Please...

JILL Just talk.

ALAN *Please!*

JILL All right, I'm going... Let me put my clothes on first.

She dresses, hastily.

ALAN You tell anyone!... Just tell and see....

JILL *Oh, stop it!* ... I wish you could believe me. It's not in the least important.

Pause.

Anyway, I won't say anything. You know that. You know I won't. . . .

Pause. He stands with his back to her.

Goodnight, then, Alan. . . . I wish – I really wish—

He turns on her, hissing. His face is distorted – possessed. In horrified alarm she turns – fumbles the door open – leaves the barn – shuts the door hard behind her, and dashes up the tunnel out of sight, past the barely visible figure of Nugget.

34

Alan stands alone, and naked.

A faint humming and drumming. The boy looks about him in growing terror.

DYSART What?

ALAN (*to Dysart*) He was there. Through the door. The door was shut, but he was there! . . . He'd seen everything. I could hear him. He was laughing.

DYSART Laughing?

ALAN (*to Dysart*) Mocking! . . . *Mocking!* . . .

Standing downstage he stares up towards the tunnel. A great silence weighs on the square.

(*to the silence: terrified*) Friend . . . Equus the Kind . . . The Merciful! . . . *Forgive me!* . . .

Silence.

It wasn't me. Not really me. *Me!* . . . Forgive me! . . . Take me back again! Please! . . . PLEASE!

He kneels on the downstage lip of the square, still facing the door, huddling in fear.

I'll never do it again. I swear . . . I swear! . . .

Silence.

(*in a moan*) *Please!!!* . . .

89

DYSART And He? What does He say?

ALAN (*to Dysart: whispering*) 'Mine!...You're mine!...I am yours and you are mine!'...Then I see his eyes. They are rolling!

Nugget begins to advance slowly, with relentless hooves, down the central tunnel.

'I see you. I see you. Always! Everywhere! Forever!'

DYSART Kiss anyone and I will see?

ALAN (*to Dysart*) Yes!

DYSART Lie with anyone and I will see?

ALAN (*to Dysart*) Yes!

DYSART And you will fail! Forever and ever you will *fail!* You will see ME – and you will FAIL!

The boy turns round, hugging himself in pain. From the sides two more horses converge with Nugget on the rails. Their hooves stamp angrily. The equus Noise is heard more terribly.

The Lord thy God is a Jealous God. He sees you. He sees you forever and ever, Alan. He sees you!...*He sees you!*

ALAN (*in terror*) Eyes!...White eyes – never closed! Eyes like flames – coming – coming!...God seest! God seest!...NO!...

Pause. He steadies himself. The stage begins to blacken.

(*quieter*) No more. No more, Equus.

He gets up. He goes to the bench. He takes up the invisible pick. He moves slowly upstage towards Nugget, concealing the weapon behind his naked back, in the growing darkness. He stretches out his hand and fondles Nugget's mask.

(*gently*) Equus...Noble Equus...Faithful and True... Godslave...Thou—God—Seest—NOTHING!

He stabs out Nugget's eyes. The horse stamps in agony. A great screaming begins to fill the theatre, growing ever louder. Alan dashes at the other two horses and blinds them too, stabbing over the rails. Their metal hooves join in the stamping.

Relentlessly, as this happens, three more horses appear in cones of light: not naturalistic animals like the first three, but dreadful creatures out of nightmare. Their eyes flare – their nostrils flare – their mouths flare. They are archetypal images – judging, punishing, pitiless. They do not halt at the rail, but invade the square. As they trample at him, the boy leaps desperately at them, jumping high and naked in the dark, slashing at their heads with arms upraised.

The screams increase. The other horses follow into the square. The whole place is filled with cannoning, blinded horses – and the boy dodging among them, avoiding their slashing hooves as best he can. Finally they plunge off into darkness and away out of sight. The noise dies abruptly, and all we hear is Alan yelling in hysteria as he collapses on the ground – stabbing at his own eyes with the invisible pick.

ALAN Find me!...Find me!...Find me!...

    KILL ME!...KILL ME!...

35

The light changes quickly back to brightness.

Dysart enters swiftly, hurls a blanket on the left bench, and rushes over to Alan. The boy is having convulsions on the floor. Dysart grabs his hands, forces them from his eyes, scoops him up in his arms and carries him over to the bench. Alan hurls his arms round Dysart and clings to him, gasping and kicking his legs in a dreadful frenzy.

Dysart lays him down and presses his head back on the bench. He keeps talking – urgently talking – soothing the agony as he can.

DYSART Here...Here...Ssssh...Ssssh...Calm now .... Lie back. *Just lie back!* Now breathe in deep. Very deep. In... Out...In...Out... That's it. ...In. *Out...In...Out...*

The boy's breath is drawn into his body with a harsh rasping sound, which slowly grows less. Dysart puts the blanket over him.

Keep it going...That's a good boy... Very good boy... It's all over now, Alan. It's all over. He'll go away now. You'll never see him again, I promise. You'll have no more bad dreams. No more awful nights. Think of that!... You are going to be well. I'm going to make you well, I promise you.... You'll be here for a while, but I'll be here too, so it won't be so bad. Just trust me...

He stands upright. The boy lies still.

Sleep now. Have a good long sleep. You've earned it...
Sleep. Just sleep... I'm going to make you well.

*He steps backwards into the centre of the square. The light brightens
some more.*

A pause.

DYSART I'm lying to you, Alan. He won't really go that easily.
Just clop away from you like a nice old nag. Oh, no! When
Equus leaves – if he leaves at all – it will be with your intes-
tines in his teeth. And I don't stock replacements... If you
knew anything, you'd get up this minute and run from me
fast as you could.

Hesther speaks from her place.

HESTHER The boy's in pain, Martin.

DYSART Yes.

HESTHER And you can take it away.

DYSART Yes.

HESTHER Then that has to be enough for you, surely?... In
the end!

DYSART (*crying out*) *All right! I'll take it away!* He'll be delivered
from madness. *What then?* He'll feel himself acceptable! *What
then?* Do you think feelings like his can be simply re-attached,
like plasters? Stuck on to other objects we select? *Look at
him!*... My desire might be to make this boy an ardent husband – a caring citizen – a worshipper of abstract and uni-
fying God. My achievement, however, is more likely to make
a ghost!... Let me tell you exactly what I'm going to do to
him!

*He steps out of the square and walks round the upstage end of it, storm-
ing at the audience.*

I'll heal the rash on his body. I'll erase the welts cut into his
mind by flying manes. When that's done, I'll set him on a
nice mini-scooter and send him puttering off into the Normal world where animals are treated *properly*: made extinct,
or put into servitude, or tethered all their lives in dim light,
just to feed it! I'll give him the good Normal world where
we're tethered beside them – blinking our nights away in a

non-stop drench of cathode-ray over our shrivelling heads! I'll take away his Field of Ha Ha, and give him Normal places for his ecstasy – multi-lane highways driven through the guts of cities, extinguishing Place altogether, *even the idea of Place!* He'll trot on his metal pony tamely through the concrete evening – and one thing I promise you: he will never touch hide again! With any luck his private parts will come to feel as plastic to him as the products of the factory to which he will almost certainly be sent. Who knows? He may even come to find sex funny. Smirky funny. Bit of grunt funny. Trampled and furtive and entirely in control. Hopefully, he'll feel nothing at his fork but Approved Flesh. *I doubt, however, with much passion!* . . . Passion, you see, can be destroyed by a doctor. It cannot be created.

He addresses Alan directly, in farewell.

You won't gallop any more, Alan. Horses will be quite safe. You'll save your pennies every week, till you can change that scooter in for a car, and put the odd fifty p on the gee-gees, quite forgetting that they were ever anything more to you than bearers of little profits and little losses. You will, however, be without pain. More or less completely without pain.

Pause.

He speaks directly to the theatre, standing by the motionless body of Alan Strang, under the blanket.

And now for me it never stops: that voice of Equus out of the cave – 'Why Me? . . . Why Me? . . . Account for Me!' . . . All right – I surrender! I say it! . . . In an ultimate sense I cannot know what I do in this place – yet I do ultimate things. Essentially I cannot know what I do – yet I do essential things. Irreversible, terminal things. I stand in the dark with a pick in my hand, striking at heads!

He moves away from Alan, back to the downstage bench, and finally sits.

I need – more desperately than my children need me – a way of seeing in the dark. What way is this? . . . *What dark is this?* . . . I cannot call it ordained of God: I can't get that far.

93

I will however pay it so much homage. There is now, in my mouth, this sharp chain. And it never comes out.

A long pause. *Image of suffering no longer*

Dysart sits staring. *The clear rightful psychomachia*

The suffering of Jesus & the same

Blackout *He cannot solve it.*

The high priest of the dream is no being sacrificed. A movement into life & suffering.

Notes

The notes in this edition are intended to serve the needs of overseas students as well as those of British-born users.

Inverted commas indicate references to stage directions.

Author's note on the book

xxiii *John Dexter:* began his career as a theatrical director with the English Stage Company in 1957 and was an Associate Director of the National Theatre in 1963–6 and 1971–5. He directed *The Royal Hunt of the Sun* at Chichester Festival Theatre in 1964.

Noh Drama: one of the classical forms of Japanese Theatre, dating from the twelfth century, highly formal and using elaborate systems of stylized gesture.

Bertholt Brecht: German dramatist (1898–1956). He made use of the traditions of folk drama to play down the naturalistic traditions of the late nineteenth-century theatre as represented by Ibsen and Shaw. Apart from *Five Finger Exercise* (1958), Shaffer's major plays have all moved away from the drawing-room.

The Royal Hunt of the Sun: Shaffer's first outstanding success, first performed at Chichester in 1964. See *Introduction*, page xii.

Black Comedy: A farce, first performed in 1965, which depends on the trick of having the actors perform as if they were in the dark, but with full lights on for the audience.

Author's notes on the play

xxv *real in a more naturalistic sense:* in *Equus*, we do not see the everyday background of the characters, except as it is filtered through Martin Dysart's memory of the case, nor

95

is the sequence of events chronological. In that sense the play is not at all naturalistic. What Shaffer means here is that he has tried to give a greater sense of everyday naturalism to the character and situation of Alan Strang by ensuring that the psychiatric details are plausible, though the play is not really best understood as a psychiatric case-book. See *Introduction*, pages xiii–xviii.

a pantomime horse: the sort of joke horse, created by two actors dressed up in a 'horse' costume, in which one performs the function of the head and forelegs, while the other – bent down – performs that of the hind quarters.

mimetically: as in a mime, a representation by movement and gesture which *suggests* the presence of objects not actually visible to the audience.

the Equus Noise: in the original production, this noise was specifically composed by Marc Wilkinson as a humming in twelve tones.

Act One

2 *subversive:* undermining Dysart's self-confidence.

3 *catatonia:* an inert state. Catatonic schizophrenia is a type of mental disorder in which the patient may remain in a state of almost complete immobility for a period of time.

Polynesian: indigenous inhabitant of one of the pacific islands. Dysart chooses it to suggest the furthest possible contrast with English.

4 *Spanish Fly:* southern European beetle from which the drug, cantharides – a substance used as an aphrodisiac or sexual stimulant – is prepared. Dysart is making a bad joke which throws Alan's actual crime into stark prominence.

6–7 *Double your pleasure ... Try the taste of Martini ... There's only one T in Typhoo ... Let's go where you wanna go – Texaco:*

advertising jingles from television commercials for chewing gum, the drink Martini, tea, and petrol.

7 *Fuck off:* see note on the language in the *Introduction*, page xix.

lav: common abbreviation for lavatory.

8 *a chief priest in Homeric Greece:* the phrase Homeric Greece refers broadly to the early period of Ancient Greek civilization from roughly 2000 to 1200 BC, the period which culminates in the conflict between the people of Mycenae and those of Troy. Their religion as far as it is understood was based on Nature and involved sacrifices, usually of animals, whose entrails were studied by the priests after the slaughter. Dysart appears to have only a popular view of the whole background to his dream. As he admits later, page 9, this Greece of his dream is a fantasy.

Mask of Agamemnon: the German archaeologist Heinrich Schlieman excavated Mycenae in 1876 and discovered the famous gold funeral masks. He wrongly supposed that he had discovered the tomb of Agamemnon, the leader of the Mycenean Greeks in the Trojan war, though archaeologists have since revealed that the tombs where the gold masks were found dated from much earlier.

the plain of Argos: Mycenae is situated on mountain slopes to the north of the plain of Argos in the eastern Peloponnese.

hieroglyphics: method of writing used in ancient Egyptian monuments and records. Words and syllables are represented by stylized miniature pictures.

9 *professional menopause:* Dysart is in his mid-forties and is suggesting that his doubts have arisen because he has reached a point in his career where he sees no development in the future. He is somewhat disillusioned and feels that his job is as petty and squalid as the priest's in his dream.

11 *if you receive my meaning:* this is the first of Frank Strang's catch-phrases, a rather false 'improvement' on the more

usual 'if you see what I mean'. Frank presumably thinks his phrase is 'posher' or more respectable.

swiz: old-fashioned children's slang for a cheat or fraud. Frank is speaking down to Alan.

it's none of my beeswax: petty euphemism for 'it's none of my business'; another of Frank's phrases which Alan is very self-conscious about.

12 *the Hammer of the Scots:* Edward I of England (1272–1307), so-called because he kept up a relentless campaign against the Scots, at that time a separate nation.

Who never smiled again?: refers to Henry I, King of England (1100–35). His only son, William, was drowned in the English Channel in 1120 and he never really recovered from the loss.

13 *Religion is the opium of the people:* Marx wrote this in the introduction to his critique of Hegel's *Philosophy of Right.*

a Sabbath evening: conventional phrase for Sunday evening in Christian societies, though the word 'Sabbath', which is derived from Hebrew and means 'day of rest', denotes Saturday in the Jewish calendar.

15 *He saith among the trumpets – Ha, Ha,:* Dora quotes from the Authorized Version of the Bible of 1611, the *Book of Job,* Chapter 39, verses 19–25. The extract comes from a section during which God speaks to Job out of a whirlwind and shows him his ignorance and foolishness. The whole passage reads:

19 Hast thou given the horse strength? hast thou clothed his neck with thunder?

20 Canst thou make him afraid as a grasshopper? the glory of his nostrils is terrible.

21 He paweth in the valley and rejoiceth in his strength: he goeth on to meet the armed men.

22 He mocketh at fear, and is not affrighted; neither turneth he back for the sword.

23 The quiver rattleth against him, the glittering

spear and the shield.

24 He swalloweth the ground with fierceness and rage: neither believeth he that it is the sound of the trumpet.

25 He saith among the trumpets, Ha, ha; and he smelleth the battle afar off, the thunder of the captains and the shouting.

The whole section is full of images of violence and blood, likely to be stimulating to Alan's imagination.

an awful lot of Westerns: films set in the so-called Wild West of the United States of America in the early period involving horseback conflicts between cowboys and Red Indians.

16 *all dressed up in bowler hat and jodhpurs!:* traditional riding dress. The bowler is a hard round hat which would give some protection in a fall; also called a derby hat. Jodhpurs are jodhpur breeches, named after a place in Rajputana in India. They are riding breeches which fit closely from knee to ankle, designed to allow better contact with the horse.

Indulging in equitation: 'posh' phrase for going riding which Alan partly resents and partly mixes with the grand language of the Bible.

17 *dosing it down the boy's throat:* Frank Strang implies that Dora was forcing religion into Alan like doses of some necessary but unpleasant medicine.

18 *an innocent man tortured to death . . .:* Frank's ironical description of the bare facts of the final sufferings of Jesus Christ. He implies that the fascination for the suffering which Christianity seems to hinge on to a non-believer is actually a sadistic sexual perversion. As he says later, 'All that stuff is just bad sex.'

I mean real kinky ones: another reference to sexual perversion. Some pictures of martyrs are sadistic in tone, especially if removed from their religious context.

19 *a higher love still:* the love of God.

21 *Double Diamond works wonders:* another television jingle, advertizing a brand of beer.

25 *Don't you be la-di-da with me:* don't treat me in a superior manner. Frank as always is very conscious of his class.

'*The Horseman skitters':* the horse jigs about in an agitated manner.

Jesse James: notorious American bandit (1847–82). The Young Horseman is being deliberately insolent to Frank.

28 *Our Lord on his way to Calvary:* Jesus Christ had to carry the cross on which he was to be crucified to the hill of Calvary. This image is very powerful in creating the identification in Alan's mind between the horse and God. Christ is chained and whipped, and so is the horse. The destruction of the picture of Christ has formed a traumatic scar in Alan's memory which is then partially healed by the picture of the horse.

31 *a loony:* slang for a madman; a colloquial shortening of 'lunatic'.

32 *There was this chain in it:* the child, Alan, sees the horse's bit as a chain.

cream dripped out: the bit was causing the horse's saliva to foam.

32–3 *Or the white horse in Revelations:* there are two white horses mentioned in the *Revelation of St John the Divine*, the final book of the New Testament of the Bible. The first is not the one referred to here but might well have appealed to Alan just as much as the second. It appears in Chapter 6, verse 2, at the opening of the first of the seven seals: 'and behold a white horse: and he that sat on him had a bow; and a crown was given unto him: and he went forth conquering, and to conquer.'

The second passage, which Alan quotes from here, is in Chapter 19, verses 11–13:

And I saw heaven opened, and behold a white horse; and he that sat upon him was called Faithful and True, and in righteousness he doth judge and make war.

His eyes were as a flame of fire, and on his head were many crowns, and he had a name written, that no man knew, but he himself.

And he was clothed with a vesture dipped in blood: and his name is called The Word of God.

33 *the most broken down old nag:* horse that is well past its working life.

gymkhana: another Indian word, like 'jodhpurs', absorbed into the world of riding; originally a meeting for athletic contests, mainly racing, now usually a meeting for show-jumping and other modern riding events.

God's got eyes everywhere: one of Dora Strang's phrases, but with special significance because it links the image of God in Alan's mind with the image of the horse on the poster which replaced the picture of Christ on His way to Calvary. As Dora says on page 29: 'It comes out all eyes'.

34 *One of those lists his mother's always reading to him:* In the early books of the Old Testament, there are frequent lists of names, family trees or genealogical tables. An early example comes from Chapter 4 of *Genesis*, verse 18, which reads: 'And unto Enoch was born Irad; and Irad begat Mehujael: and Mehujael begat Methusael; and Methusael begat Lamech', and so on. These lists sometimes run to very great lengths.

Prince begat Prance: Alan's own quasi-biblical genealogy of Equus is a tissue of words drawn from his obsession with horses mixed up with his sexual repression. Some of the words link by sound association and some by sense. Prince (the name of the horse in his mother's story) suggests the sound of Prance, which is also the high-stepping action of horses. This leads to Prankus, which not only links the sound of Prance to Flankus which follows, but also suggests that Alan's activities are naughty, a prank. Flankus reminds us of the body of the horse, the flank, the part

101

which is whipped by the rider, and that leads easily by sound and sense to Spankus. This suggests both a naughty child being punished and the more general idea of flagellation as a perverted means of achieving sexual arousal. The next name, Spunkus the Great, confirms the masturbatory nature of Alan's fantasies. It is the climax of the list at this point; 'spunk' being a slang word, commonly used by boys for semen. The next sequence reverts to the body of the horse and leads through the vowel sound to the name Equus itself. Fleckwus refers to the flecks of spit on the horse's neck and recalls the child Alan's experience with Trojan and the 'cream' dripping from his bits. ('Cream' is another slang word for semen.) When he reaches Equus, Alan refers to him as 'my only begotten son' the words normally applied to Christ as the only begotten Son of God. 'Fleckwus' speaks these words, so that the sexual element of the fantasy is tightly interwoven with the religious element.

35 *chinkle-chankle:* in Alan's fantasy, the word for the horse's bit.

Ek...wus: Dysart, somewhat belatedly, realizes what the noises Alan made in his dreams earlier (page 10) refer to.

'Alan, in mime, begins to thrash himself': Alan's flagellation unites again his religious fantasy with his sexual repression. Flagellation has been used both in religious devotion as a suppression or mortification of the desires of the flesh, and also to revive flagging sexual activity.

37 *I haven't the aptitude:* Alan is using his father's phrases. Aptitude is another of the words which Frank Strang would use in an effort to give a more refined impression.

38 *Philco ... Remington ... Robex ... Croydex ... Volex ... Pifco ... Beautiflor ... Windolene ... Hoover:* brand names of various household goods.

41 *dandy:* very stiff brush used in grooming horses, sometimes made of split whalebone, or very stiff vegetable fibre.

curry-comb: a metal comb used in grooming horses.

45 *if you're kinky for Northern Hygienic:* if you have a particular fancy for brisk and efficient Northern women – by implication this would be a strange liking.

the sacred acrobats of Crete: another allusion to Dysart's interest in ancient Greece. A legend exists that Athens paid a tribute of young men and women to the civilization centred on Knossos on the island of Crete. In the legend, these were to be sacrificed to the Minotaur, or bull-headed monster, who lived in the labyrinth below the palace of Knossos. Archaeology has indicated that the bull was indeed worshipped in Knossos and that there were festivals of bull-dancing not dissimilar from some modern Mediterranean bull-running, in which young men show their bravery by jumping between the horns of a chàrging bull and then over its back.

The Highland Games: athletic gathering in Scotland. There is again heavy irony here on the word 'norrmal' which not only makes fun of Margaret Dysart's Scottish accent, but implies that her judgment is not very sound: since, for example, a sport such as 'tossing the caber' – which involves hurling poles of wood the size of telegraph poles as far as possible – is hardly any more 'normal' than jumping through the horns of running bulls.

46 *the Iliad:* one of the two epic poems by the ancient Greek poet, Homer, which tells the story of the Trojan war.

the Gorbals: very poor area of Glasgow.

a Shrink: colloquial name for a psychiatrist, from 'head-shrinker'.

some drizzly kirk: rain-soaked church: kirk is a Scottish word for church.

some Doric temple: Greek temple of the earliest type. This does however betray Dysart's rather popular view of Greek pre-history. His interests are mainly, as he says, in Homeric Greece – but the Greeks of this period, who are called Achaeans, did not build the temples which we traditionally associate with Ancient Greece. After the decline of Mycenean civilization, Greece was invaded from the north by a people called the Dorians, and it is they who built the first and simplest type of temple, which is accordingly called Doric.

clouds tearing through pillars – eagles bearing prophecies out of the sky: references to Greek mythology. The eagle was frequently associated with Zeus, the highest of the Greek gods, who used clouds as disguises or tricks.

four bottles of Chianti ... condiment donkeys labelled Sally and Peppy: Dysart refers derisively to traditional and rather vulgar souvenirs. Chianti is a popular Italian wine; and *condiment donkeys* are models of donkeys used as salt and pepper containers, hence the names.

a thousand local Gods: as well as the great gods – Zeus, Apollo, Poseidon – there were in the ancient religions any number of minor divinities, among them – as Dysart says – *Geniuses*, or spirits of place.

an Everest of papers: enormous mountain of papers; work still to be done.

47 *Touché:* term used in fencing when one of the combatants, having been touched by the tip of his opponent's sword, succeeds in scoring a return hit. Dysart means that Hesther has replied effectively to his challenge on the word 'normal'.

51 *His Holy of Holies?:* his inner sanctuary. In the Old Testament, the term refers to the most holy part of the temple where only the high priest may enter.

brush him with many brushes: Biblical phrasing which Dysart uses to play along with Alan's fantasy.

55 *The Ark of the Manbit:* another parody phrase, recalling the Ark of the Convenant in the Old Testament.

56 *His ribs are of ivory:* recalls the language of the Biblical *Song of Solomon*, in which the love of King Solomon and the Queen of Sheba is celebrated. Chapter 5, verse 14 reads:

His hands are as gold rings set with beryl: his belly is as
bright ivory overlaid with sapphires.
His legs are as pillars of marble, set upon sockets of fine
gold.

His Last Supper: refers to the Passover Supper which
Christ celebrated with his disciples before the crucifixion.
Each of these phrases strongly suggests Alan's only partial
and fragmentary understanding of the words he is using.

57 *His neck comes out of my body:* although to Alan this phrase
means the unification of himself with the horse, it is also
an arresting and grotesque phallic image, reinforcing the
sexual suggestiveness of the whole scene and the focus of
Alan's obsession.

Act Two

60 *a frozen tango dancer:* the tango was a popular ballroom
dance of the 1950s and requires somewhat exaggerated
postures from the dancers.
the black cave of the Psyche: the word 'psyche' means 'mind'
in Greek and is the source of our word psychiatrist. Dysart
refers here to the inner recesses of the mind which we normally repress.

64 *a con trick:* confidence trick, in which the crook wins his
victim's confidence before robbing or tricking him or her
in some other way.
truth drugs: some modern drugs have been supposed to put
the subject into a trance during which he or she cannot
prevent him or herself from telling the truth.

65 *placebo:* means, in Latin, 'I shall please'. The word is
nowadays used for a medicine which has no real curative
power but helps the patient by satisfying a desire to be
given something to take for his or her symptoms.

67 *finicky:* fussy.

lowest sperm count: having the smallest number of spermatozoa in his semen, and therefore little chance of fathering a child.

Peleponnese: the name given to the southern part of mainland Greece, south of the isthmus of Corinth.

Fiats: mass-produced Italian cars.

Kao-Pectate: medical preparation for curing diarrhoea.

centaurs: mythical creatures each possessing the head and trunk of a man connected to the body and legs of a horse.

68 *Kodachrome snaps:* 'snaps' is short for 'snapshots', a colloquial word for photographs. Kodachrome is a brand name of a type of colour film.

Dionysus: the Greek god of fertility, and in ancient times the central figure of some of the most passionate and violent sexual rituals. Alan's experience is, in a way, Dionysiac.

71 *the Hallelujah Chorus:* the famous and popular chorus from Handel's oratorio *Messiah*, frequently referred to, as here, in a jokey way.

74 *without a bean:* without any money.

dates: evenings out with boyfriends.

76 *skinflick:* sex film. Films are colloquially called 'flicks' from the early days when the frames were not in such close sequence as they are now and a flickering effect occurred; 'skinflick' suggests the type of picture in which the performers would be for the most part naked.

all those heavy Swedes: this is somewhat unfair to Swedes nowadays; but Sweden did acquire, in the 1950s, a reputation for being more sexually uninhibited than much of the rest of Europe, and many sex films were made there.

90 *The Lord thy God is a Jealous God:* the God of the Old Testament, Jehovah, is depicted as a much more punishing figure than the God of the New Testament.

'archetypal images': images of horses out of some original creative source, beyond the physical horse we know.

92 *puttering off:* driving off. The word is meant to suggest the

noise made by the scooter.

93 *cathode-ray:* television: the cathode-ray tube is the princi-
pal component in a television set.

the odd fifty p on the gee-gees: an occasional fifty pence bet on
a horse race.

Follow-up work and questions for discussion

(See also questions included in the Introduction, page xii–xix).

Some things to do

1 Sketch a ground plan of the set and auditorium for *Equus*. What is the point of having the audience upstage? Why do the cast sit on upstage benches throughout? How is the space used to suggest the various locations?

2 Consider Dysart's addresses to the audience and his conversations with Hesther separately. What do we learn from them that we do not learn from the rest of the play?

3 The play works like a detective story towards the answer to the question, not *Whodunnit?* but *Why he dunnit?* Work out the stages of Dysart's investigation. Is it too calculated? Isn't he a bit slow identifying the noise Alan makes in his sleep?

Some unanswerable questions

1 What do we mean by 'normal'?

2 Why are our secret, our private, and our public lives seldom at one?

3 What do we mean by 'passion' and 'worship'?

4 Is the intensity of Alan's experience possible without some kind of violence?

5 Is some sort of guilt inescapable in the context of sex and religion?

6 Shaffer's world is largely without 'love'. Would 'love' in any sense make any difference?